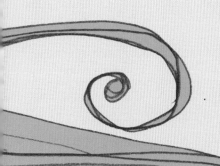

IMAGEMAKERS

cutting edge fashion illustration

MARTIN DAWBER

MITCHELL BEAZLEY

First published in Great Britain in 2004 by Mitchell Beazley,
an imprint of Octopus Publishing Group Ltd
2–4 Heron Quays, London E14 4JP

Reprinted 2004

ISBN 1 84000 983 7

A CIP catalogue copy of this book is available
from the British Library

To order this book as a gift or incentive, contact
Mitchell Beazley on 020 7531 8481

Commissioning Editor **Hannah Barnes-Murphy**

Executive Art Editor **Auberon Hedgecoe**

Project Editor **Emily Asquith**

Design **John Round Design**

Production **Seyhan Esen**

Jacket illustration **Orange Juice, Satoshi Matsuzawa, 2003**
Half title page **Legs, Claire Anderson, 2003**
Title page **Baiser, Marguerite Sauvage, 2003**
This page **Stick up Kids, Anthony Kolber, 2002**
Contents page **Redman, Anthony Kolber, 2002**

Set in Oberon, Din, and Ronda ITC
Produced by Toppan Printing Co. (HK) Ltd
Printed and bound in China

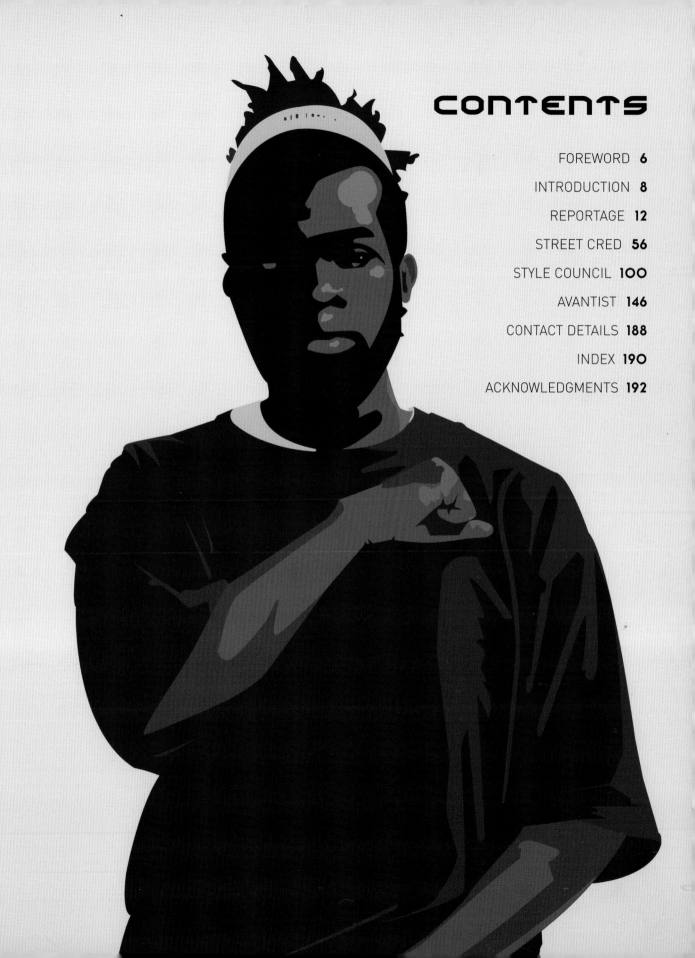

CONTENTS

FOREWORD

I'm not sure if I would describe myself as a Fashion Illustrator, but perhaps as something wider than that. The dominating subject of my work is people and lifestyle – real or imagined – be it idling lotus-eaters gazing out over a city from penthouse apartments, happy couples, or snatches of street and club life. It's how clothes, possessions, and music define personalities that fascinates me. Sometimes I find myself creating back-stories for some of the characters, working out how they got here. Influences are many and varied: Jasper Johns, David Hockney, Alberto Giacometti, Japanese prints, contemporary illustrators, fashion, design, architecture, and music – just about everything is relevant.

I am forever tearing things out of newspapers and magazines. It all ferments down into a rich compost that keeps ideas growing. As a kid I collected US comics and I must be regressing, as I am still interested in contemporary comic-book art, especially Manga and European comics.

The job of an illustrator is to make an arresting image that fulfils the client's brief. It's a commercial enterprise. I think an illustrator's most important skills are the ability to work quickly under pressure – when you're hung-over, your girlfriend has dumped you, or Arsenal are running away with the league. Also, never be surprised by a client – instead face the challenge and create the best image possible in order to help sell the product. Fashion illustration's continuing success is, in part, due to its flexibility. It can poke fun at fashion victims or make them beautiful creatures worthy of admiration. It can make modern life look rubbish, or sprinkle trendy fairy-dust on the blandest of products!

Gavin Reece

Fashion is a chameleon, and the current scene is as much an expression of thoughts and emotions as it is about shape and silhouette. Fashion has always proved to be a reflection of the times, expressing itself both as part of history and part of the present. It is not a whimsical mannerism but an exciting addition to our lives, with a purpose and focus, which it is the illustrator's business to interpret and represent.

The standard of fashion drawing today is extremely high, and the position and regard of the illustrator is steadily increasing. It is widely recognised that an illustration can sell a product just as successfully as a photographic image. Fashion illustration is no longer limited to sketching a garment or technically explaining its construction. To be 100% true-to-life is not a full interpretation. Often the illustrator will purposefully ignore realism and describe an idealized version of the design. Exaggeration is part of fashion. Artistic licence is essential. Playing to the senses gives the image more impact – it retains the excitement of fashion.

The 51 illustrators featured within these pages paint a brilliantly executed and visually stimulating picture of the international fashion scene today.

Jasper Conran

FEMME FATALE ALANNA CAVANAGH 2002

BACK IN THE DAY ANTON STOREY 2002

INTRODUCTION

Fashion illustration is currently enjoying a renaissance that fully embraces the latest creative media while also cherishing its rich and resonant heritage. Today's new illustrators draw the clothes and paint the faces of contemporary life in a variety of styles and techniques, which echo the breadth of their vibrant culture. The 51 illustrators featured in this book represent this exciting, emerging talent.

What is the difference between fashion drawing and fashion illustration? Fashion drawing will always remain the technical sketch that imparts practical information. It breaks down the image into purely industrial components of construction. It appeals to the intellect. Like an architect's plan, it exists as a blueprint, to aid in the construction and assembly of a garment. It has a practical function.

Fashion illustration, on the other hand, provides a pictorial expansion that plays directly on our emotions and appeals more to the heart than the head. It subtly conveys far more information than a schematic drawing will ever do, but this is not necessarily achieved by showing detail. More often than not, fashion illustrations work by suggestion – they play upon our senses. These are emotive works that powerfully expand on style and content. Just like the images in well-remembered childhood storybooks, these illustrations weave their magic spell by creating an evocative personal interpretation and appearance. Those that construct a narrative around characters increase our reaction to the composition.

Fashion and its related images now flood our media and culture. There has been increased interest in contemporary fashion with retrospectives on Versace, Armani, and Westwood, to name a few, now travelling the world's galleries and museums. There have been celebrations of style in dress with *Radical Fashion* (V&A, London) *Skin Tight* (Museum of Contemporary Art, Chicago) and *Les sixties, mode d'emploi* (Musée de la Mode et du Textile, Paris); and showcases acknowledging the radical trends of current fashion photographers and stylists such as Guy Bourdin, Nick Knight, and David LaChapelle. Yet the recent surge in inventive fashion illustration being practised by college graduates remains uncharted and is rarely seen outside their workplace.

Fashion illustration has always existed on a legacy of stylized sophistication. It stems from the celebrated 1920s and '30s *Vogue* and *Harper's Bazaar* covers by Barbier and Erté right through to the undisputed craftsmanship of René Gruau, who characterized the 1940s and '50s in his notable *L'Officiel* and *International Textiles* covers, and into the 1980s with Antonio Lopez, who dominated fashion illustration with his work for both *Vanity Fair* and *Elle*. When fashion illustration was elbowed out of the glossies by the photographer and his stylist during the middle of the last century, it forced the illustrator to take a back seat in favour of the *vérité* of the camera lens.

However, the illustrator has been reinstated as a fabricator of style following the shift from pure fashion

TRANSIT MARCOS CHIN 2002

PAMPER YOURSELF NATHALIE DION 2003

journalism to a more general lifestyle journalism, apparent in the influx of the style magazines such as *Wallpaper**, *Clear,* and *Surface* that arrived during the 1990s. All at once, everything from personal gadgets to fitted kitchens was afforded a visual treatment preciously guarded as the reserve of the latest Paris fashion. Being in fashion was as much about your attitude toward what mobile phone you owned or what car you drove as to which designer shoes you wore. Fashion imagery seemed to devour every type of visual media available.

Illustration had until this point been snubbed by the advertising world as outmoded and archaic, only dusted down when cartooning was the order of the day, so it was like a breath of fresh air when the pseudo-realistic illustrations of British graphic artists Jason Brooks and Jasper Goodall started to appear in magazines (*Vogue, Big, Arena,* and *Visionaire,* etc.) in the late '90s, and caused an editorial stir in *The Guardian, The Independent,* and *The Sunday Times.* These new illustrators were well positioned to conjure contemporary lifestyle images by using illustration techniques that now appeared highly original after their lengthy absence from the scene.

The inventively rendered women of self-styled artist Julie Verhoeven or the snapshots of urban street-life depicted by Gavin Reece or Graham Rounthwaite attest to the spirit of fashion illustration that has lately reasserted itself in the documentation of fashionable style. (Graham was responsible for the

100 Adobe Photoshop-generated characters that peopled Levi's late '90s US ad campaign.) Their images are the new barometers of popular culture.

The present kudos afforded to fashion illustration has been long overdue. The discarded fashion plates of yesterday are now being replaced by increasingly sought-after illustrations which are valued in their own right as collectable pieces of art. It is no longer unheard of for fashion illustrators to receive portrait commissions as an alternative to the traditional oil study. Now that the barriers between the disciplines of Fine Arts and Applied Design no longer exist, artists are keen to exploit previously restricted techniques.

The intention of *Imagemakers* is to provide an appraisal of these emerging trends in fashion illustration. Its focus is the remarkably rich work by art-school and college graduates from across the world. Their belated challenge to the stereotypical "long-legged Lolitas" of previous generations of illustrators is innovative and experimental, arising from the ever-widening media palette that is now available to them.

It is refreshing to see these current practitioners of fashion illustration testing established traditions and techniques in a manner that remained all but unrecognized up until a decade ago. They achieve this not only by their exploitation of new creative media, but also through the synergy of the traditional craft-orientated disciples with their digital counterparts to evolve an entirely new formula and language for representing fashion. They are developing their own individual way of portraying fashion and lifestyle.

The onset of more advanced and sophisticated computer software added further tools to the illustrator's paintbox and has brought an advance in style technique as pioneering as the arrival of camera and film. The explosion of the Web has provided not only an information-gathering highway that makes everything accessible with the click of a mouse, but also provided a new platform for the exploitation and presentation of fashion. The traditional values of elitism, symptomatic of fashion's rarified ivory tower of exclusivity, have been forced to submit to the volume of traffic on the internet. To engage with this creative media is to open the doors to a global audience that previously would have been excluded from stepping inside. Interestingly, several of the featured illustrators have previously only worked within a virtual canvas.

It is important to mention that all of these artists come from the generation that saw the groundbreaking challenges that popular music and street-style fashion brought to the domain of haute couture. For the last 20 years, fashion has ceased to be within the absolute control of the remaining fashion elite. Popular culture saw a reversal of the process by which fashion is "made", with established fashion labels taking their reference from the dress codes of real people out on the street, which permitted music and youth styles to influence the previously out-of-touch ateliers.

Previous street tribes such as beatniks, mods and rockers, and hippies had established that style could be instigated by young people out on their own street catwalks rather than by the remote diktats of a fashion guru. Beginning in the mid-1970s, punk's anti-fashion creed, initiated on London's King's Road, was eagerly exploited by Zandra Rhodes in her cleaned-up revamps of their aggressive safety-pin and torn T-shirt uniform. Equally alternative, the short lived "grunge" look, typified in the early 1990s by the mandatory ripped jeans and oversized sweaters (the progeny of rock bands Nirvana and Pearl Jam) shocked both sides of the Atlantic when Perry Ellis and Christian Lacroix adapted it for their collections, to the consternation of established clients. Instead of dictating style, they had been forced to digest it.

At about the same time, British magazines, *i-D* and *The Face*, flew in the face of accepted values in the fashion world and toyed with a level of editorial and image-making that had previously been kept underground by the accepted glossies. The arrival of magazines such as *Dazed & Confused* and *Tank*, ten years later, secured a conduit for promoting the cutting-edge iconography that currently saturates today's scene.

In a continuation of the theme, the rarified salon catwalk show increasingly became more like a rock concert or cabaret in an ever-continuing battle to stimulate senses that were becoming accustomed to a visual representation that knew no bounds. The media soon followed, turning its cameras on

ONLY DANCING MONICA HELLSTROM 2003

GIRL WITH RED HAIR ANOUSHKA MATUS 2002

the street catwalks, with TV stations MTV and Pop Eye recording the unpredictable face of fashion.

It is not only media and music stars, but also, incredibly, even footballers who are now able to start iconic trends that have cloned whole groups of fashion victims. The reality of buying into a fashionable lifestyle has become increasingly more possible, and the aesthetic values of the consumer have become heightened by a culture that constantly promotes visual awareness.

The illustrators featured in this book are recent graduates who represent their industry's new blood. Both conceptual and provocative, their work often bursts through the restrictions of the conventional representations of fashion. For them illustration is no longer about the myth of the blemish-free fashion ideal that is still projected from one glossy mainstream magazine cover to the next. Instead, they are out to rejuvenate the orthodox consumer image. Prescriptive boundaries are continually being redefined in their contemporary realization of style and fashion.

Importantly, the works that are shown here document the illustrators individual and personal observations on the prevailing fashion scene. These artists are not being commissioned to report on the rarified catwalk creations still offered each season on the runways of the fashion world. Some of the featured illustrators don't even wish to pigeonhole themselves as fashion illustrators. Their commentary is much wider in scope; their supply of information is the world around them. Their source of reference is the everyday, from billboard advertisements to music videos, packaging, and must-have design objects, which all now come with their own memorable visual tag-lines. All seem subconsciously absorbed and stored for future exploitation. Comfortably in tune with their own cultures and lifestyle, and the embellished visual environment that they now inhabit, it is this that feeds their creative imaginations.

By publishing these new illustrators in the format of a sourcebook, the intention is to offer a welcome display of their creativity rather than a "how-to" manual. *Imagemakers* is presented as a record to inform and inspire its readers.

This book is laid out in four broad chapters: Reportage; Street Cred; Style Council; and Avantist. Each section groups together a variety of illustrators who share a common approach, aim, interest, or theme. Together these illustrators, either by their subject matter or style of presentation, all have something pertinent to say about today's lifestyle. They represent the imagemakers.

ZIP UP YUKO SHIMIZU 2002

DRAG QUEEN KNUD SARAH BEETSON 2002

Ever since man followed his primal urge to scratch a likeness of his world on a cave wall, there has been an increasingly evocative lineage of documentation capturing the ever-shifting patterns of progress. The Egyptians were the first to impart a decorative stylization to their representations of life around them. Centuries later, these distinctive depictions are still acclaimed as the perfect union of style with technique.

This fascination with capturing society and the clothes that people wore has been chronicled by succeeding centuries through paintings and drawings that catalogue lifestyle and manners. Most of this information has been gleaned from the obsession with portraiture of the rich and famous. However, freedom of expression by individual artists was often limited, since most were dependent on pleasing the benefactor commissioning the work.

Master craftsmen developed styles and techniques that have successively classified art throughout the centuries. These captured likenesses remain accessible as an enduring record of the modes of society that still fascinates and resonates today out of the pages of *Life* and *Hello!* magazines.

In the 20th century, photography gave rise to a means of capturing real life that was within the reach

of more people. The availability of affordable cameras in the 1950s meant everyone could snap away and be guaranteed some kind of authentic result. The art of reportage now assumed the mantle of a pastime.

Over the entire precious heritage is suspended the question of trustworthiness. Are all these records reliable and true, or are they a stylized falsehood? To what extent did each reporter of events allow their representation to be coloured by either skill or subjectivity? In the end, just how aligned to authentic representation is ability and technique?

Similarly, how plausible are the scenes that the Bayeux Tapestry needleworkers described with their embroidered comic-strip technique? Did Elizabethan England really resemble the mannered portraits of Hans Holbein? How fabricated was the nostalgic world of Norman Rockwell? Probably none of these were truly authentic. What these artisans captured was a personal tribute within their own style and times. They were, first and foremost, imagemakers.

In today's visually obsessive culture, coverage is often passed around like visual Chinese whispers. The falsification of the truth continues to be re-packaged to appeal to each viewer. Authenticity seems ever more elusive from a society that continues to refuse to

distinguish fact from fiction. "Tell it like is" is no longer considered a viable option because there is a constant demand for window dressing. Everything from a simple pair of Levi jeans through to the funeral of a princess is styled to appeal to its own target audience as another piece of visual merchandise. And just as the intrusion into the home by television blurred the edges of stark realism, by bringing everything from war to moon-landings as close as "made-for-TV" programming, today the virtual screen of the Web fosters a portrayal of the world unhindered by any form of reality check.

Illustration has always lent itself to this type of fabrication by nature of its variety and stylization, and the free reign of the illustrator's imagination. The expression of a particular illustrator may not appeal to everyone, but it can't be ignored in its value as a personal take on life.

The same applies to the 13 illustrators gathered in this section. Their reportage on contemporary lifestyle attempts to hold up a mirror to the current scene. Drawing upon their own personal experiences and encounters, through their individual and personal handwriting, they continue to express themselves with illustrations that convincingly document present-day life, its characters, and its sense of style.

MARGUERITE SAUVAGE

FRANCE

UNIVERSITE PARIS 8 VINCENNES-ST-DENIS, FRANCE

IFP, UNIVERSITE PARIS II PANTHEON-ASSAS, FRANCE

After specializing in semiology for her Masters in Information and Communication, Marguerite seems more than adequately equipped to read and present current culture. She relies on a pastel palette to bring life to her characters in a delightful, expressively tonal style. Initially hand drawn as pencil sketches, her images are then inked in and scanned into the computer to be enhanced using Adobe Photoshop and Illustrator software. Her imagination is a melting pot of all that surrounds her in life. The seductive over-the-shoulder stare of the redhead, with her Manga comic-book eyes and active hair, lures the viewer like a young Bardot. The ecstatic disturbance caused by the boy band (overleaf) is captured by the simple mass formation of the outstretched silhouette of arms from their attentive female audience. The assemblies of shoppers (overleaf) are framed both laterally and vertically. These busy scenes present a kaleidoscope of rhythm and pattern as figures cross the page in pursuit of their shopping spree.

I don't really know if I draw fashion illustrations or not. I only wonder about it when people tell me I do. The pictures I produce are "fashionable." I'm glad to catch a glimpse of contemporary life. That is the main purpose of my images. That also explains why characters are so important in my work — people that express a lifestyle by themselves, their attitudes. I love faces, I love bodies. Fashion is for me a way to emphasize them. To be honest I just like giving people eye candy.

WALK
DONT
WALK

ANOUSHKA MATUS

UK/SWITZERLAND
BASEL SCHOOL OF DESIGN, SWITZERLAND

There is a wry humour in Anoushka's sketches that knowingly categorizes its subject; a rebellious streak that has all the spontaneity and naïve appeal of children's art. Outlined as single-line doodles, these vignettes make use of a consciously flippant caricature of the female figure which is both enchanting and amusing. Although these simple tracings are expressed with a sharp eye and wit, they are not grotesque cartoons that point a critical finger at today's lifestyle. Rather they represent the confidence of the woman of today who is not afraid to speak her mind. Anoushka articulates this message with the simplest line drawing, which is then scanned to be coloured and textured using Adobe Photoshop. Manipulation of colour and texture is kept to a minimum, and skin tone is suggested rather than applied. Colour is block stencilled and does not stretch beyond three variants. Her artistry represents a shrewd comment – not a comic joke – expressed in a language that the viewer can instantly identify with.

VELOGARAGE ADVERTISEMENT FOR A BICYCLE REPAIR SHOP 2003

I might not actually have a lap-dog, but I imagine I'd look pretty good with one. "That" spring/summer '04 Prada dress my budget isn't going to allow, well the lucky girl on my illustration got it. I release all my styling fantasies on them.

TRACY ZHOU

CHINA

FINE ARTS INSTITUTE OF SHANGHAI UNIVERSITY, CHINA
NORTHWESTERN POLYTECHNIC UNIVERSITY, CALIFORNIA, USA

Tracy's seated, faceless females have a relaxed cubist form and appear to persistently question the viewer. Before working on the canvas, Tracy carries out a series of coloured preparatory sketches. Her restrained style of oil painting demonstrates leanings toward the mysticism of Giorgio de Chirico and Carlo Carrà. These enigmatic women are balanced within the canvas, sphinx-like, waiting for the viewer to answer their riddle. Facial features are left blank to heighten the sense of mystery. Naturally posed, with legs crossed, they balance on austere chairs and sofas, in full control of the situation. With little else to visually disturb the composition, there is an amplification of contentment and serenity.

Sometimes my friends ask me, "Why are Picasso's artworks the best?" There is no answer to that question. Likewise I believe that there are no rules for beauty or fashion, because they are just those things that make you feel good, that feel right.

KERSTIN WACKER

GERMANY

MODEKOLLEG HOLZENBECHER, STUTTGART, GERMANY

Using traditional techniques, Kerstin starts with a pencil sketch that is worked up with coloured crayons, markers, and Indian ink. The computer is only employed when considering backgrounds. She confesses that she is not a "one-shot" worker and takes considerable time developing the initial sketch and paying attention to details, before arriving at the final illustration. Kerstin's figures stride across the page with the confidence of people that know their own mind. There is real drive in these stretched silhouettes. Her fragile females are birdlike in appearance, with stalk-like legs that contradict human anatomy. This graphic stylization has affinities with Alberto Giacometti's emaciated sculpting of the human body. The constant pull toward consumerism in today's culture is characterized by the addition of overstated, gaily coloured bags. These inflated artifacts have become an essential trapping of the profile of contemporary dress. They are no longer just practical accessories, but represent the spoils of retail warfare and are touted like banners proclaiming these women as the victors of the fight.

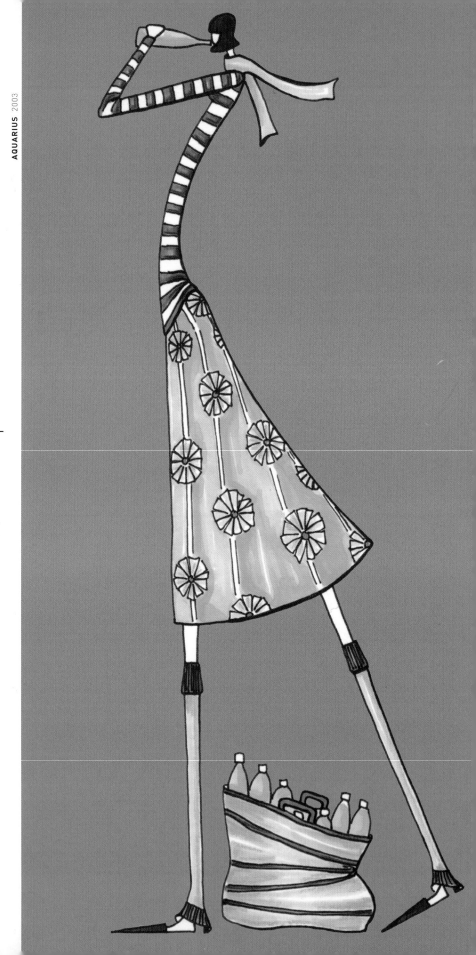

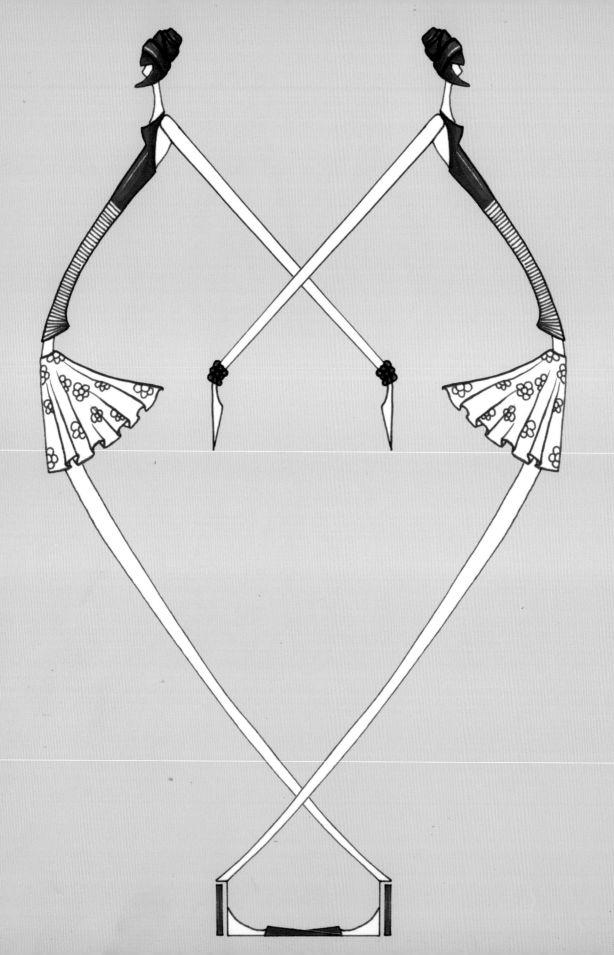

Being a very visual person, I love living in different places and being exposed to unexpected impressions. Much of the fun in my work comes from exploring different cultures, eras, and moods. I always have my sketchbook with me, to put down whatever is inspiring me. For me, fashion is the perfect vehicle to transform my inspiration into something real. Although my drawings are very precise, I work very spontaneously – no conceptual principles, no hidden messages to be discovered. I don't want to be provocative – I like my illustrations to be nice and charming. When I'm drawing I'm almost lost in my own world... a good feeling!

SILBERBLICK 2003

NATHALIE DION

CANADA
CONCORDIA UNIVERSITY, MONTREAL, CANADA

Nathalie's delicately executed illustrations capture situations by ingeniously trapping the moment on the page, creating brief snapshots of everyday life. She is constantly looking for source material; sometimes it comes from the architecture around her, other times from flipping through old books from a garage sale. Sketching her textures and patterns in watercolour or gouache, she recomposes them using Adobe Photoshop. Nathalie's beanpole people appear to be carved like ancient Egyptian tomb-reliefs. The sheer exuberance of succumbing to the temptation of purchasing a new pair of shoes is captured in the slender balletic pose of the figure opposite. She almost dances with joy, stretching on points, at the prospect of her intended acquisition. Overleaf, two females attempt to stare each other out while the pinstriped object of their desire looks on, unsure of the final outcome. The distinction of the two contenders is well delineated in their modes of dress. The tightly wound black bun and all-encompassing tonal clothes of one contrasts with the free cascading auburn hair and cropped outfit of the other, holding her fluted glass of temptation. What will happen next is left tantalizingly uncertain.

For me, fashion is above all a matter of attitude, charisma, presence... and humour. My characters are never of the latest fashion; they are contemporary and timeless. The essence is in their demeanour, their gesture, their finesse.

THE SWIMMER 2003

THE SHADOW SEEKER 2003

BEN TAN

USA

UNIVERSITY OF CALIFORNIA, LOS ANGELES, USA

Ben's ladies toy with the viewer with their manipulative, if playful, innocence and erotic overtones. These are the flirts of today's culture that represent a prankish "look but don't touch" sensibility. Their body language is saucily reminiscent of the naïvety of 1940s' soft porn. Alberto Vargas's pulp fiction femme-fatales could be their predecessors. Today these young vamps have an innocence that seduces the viewer with a stimulating, in-your-face posturing. This one pouts and sulks like a Lolita-esque schoolgirl; another holds our attention, frozen like a burglar caught red-handed, illuminated in the light of a refrigerator. Ben does not shy away from controversial themes. Using the simplest of blocked colour, the image of Kate (overleaf) forcefully registers an underlying sense of tragedy in her disturbed black hair and dress. Preferring the flexibility, Ben sketches directly onto the computer using a Wacom Intuos tablet and Adobe Painter. He establishes a basic pose from a photographic reference, then works up the other details.

MIRROR 2003

CAUGHT 2001

For me, good fashion illustration, like any good illustration,
needs to evoke an emotional response from the viewer.
That feeling becomes the core story of the piece, and
everything else around it, colours, form, pose, facial
expression, media, textures, linework, clothes, and
accessories, need to work together to sell that story.

GWEN KERAVAL

FRANCE
ECOLE EMILE COHL, LYON, FRANCE

Gwen's restrained computer graphic illustrations present an encapsulated expression of contemporary life, beautifully crafted in simple line and muted colour. Computer enhancements are applied as sensitively as any paint or gouache, and the restrained treatment of the colour palette is delightfully emotional rather than representational. The tenderness of each scene is frozen by harmonious and complementary tones, while the narrative is realized with a minimum of effort – nothing is superfluous or excessive. Gwen's execution focuses on the power of the minimal gesture to reach out and touch the heart of the viewer: the star-crossed lovers' first tiff; the tentative approaches of commitment; the trust that follows passion. All these are sensitively conveyed with the ease of a graphic novel's minimal line and content.

VESPA BOY *LOLIE* 2002

LOLITA *LOLIE* 2002

It is now much easier to experiment graphically. It is also easier to access a wider choice of images thanks to the internet. It has created a sort of global fusion that forces everyone to go farther, to push boundaries. It's an infinite pool of inspiration.

Often combining photographs with her own drawings to form a montage, Christiane humorously conveys our fascination with what we eat through this series of picture postcards that document current food fixations and obsessions. Preferring her own organic pencil or felt-tip lines, Christiane scans these into the computer rather than using a digital tablet. Her figures resemble characters in search of their own cartoon series. Each one employs the characteristics of a Hanna-Barbera toon-flic character and

seems to be speaking to us directly from the page. The food and the girls' racial characteristics are captured by economy of line and technique. The cross-cultural foodstuff becomes a fashion accessory, saying as much about the character as the clothes that they wear or the hairstyles they sport. This is nouvelle couture. The fact that none are even faintly overweight says as much about the their fixation on maintaining their gymnasium lifestyles as their obvious enjoyment of food.

TOKYO 2003

LONDON 2003

Fashion seems meaningless without people. Only people, their lives and their stories, make it into something individual, but all by itself it becomes meaningless. This is why I like to show people and fashion in a humorous context or within a story.

YUKO SHIMIZU

USA/JAPAN
WASEDA UNIVERSITY, TOKYO, JAPAN
SCHOOL OF VISUAL ARTS, NEW YORK, USA

Yuko initially draws with a Japanese brush and Indian ink on paper, then scans the drawing into her G4 laptop where she adds colour in Adobe Photoshop. She prefers to keep the figure and the background on separate layers in case of revisions. Following lots of figure-drawing classes, Yuko confidently represents the body in increasingly weird perspectives, and continues researching unfamiliar areas. Her expressive, clean-cut line delineates the female form with an economy of execution and technique. This spare style is beautifully maintained by the considered framing of each figure on the page. Yuko captures an almost Kitagawa Utamaro wood-cut simplicity in describing her seductive outline. There is a forthright attitude that helps promote each theme to its full value, but although the subject matter could spill over into humour or lewdness, this is carefully avoided by the elegance and style of her execution.

X-X-SHORT, X-SMALL *LETTERS OF DESIRE* 2002

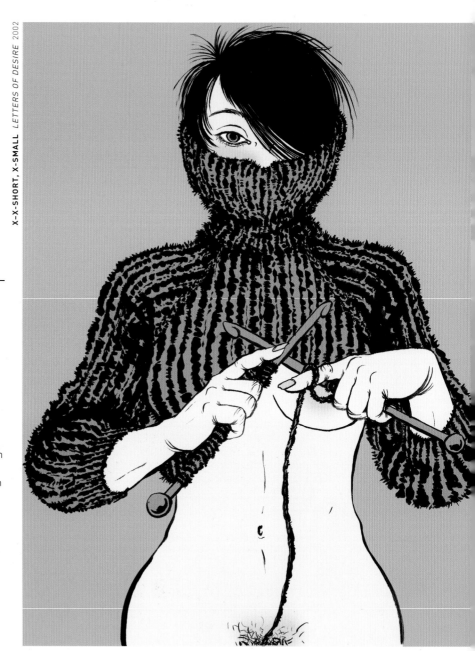

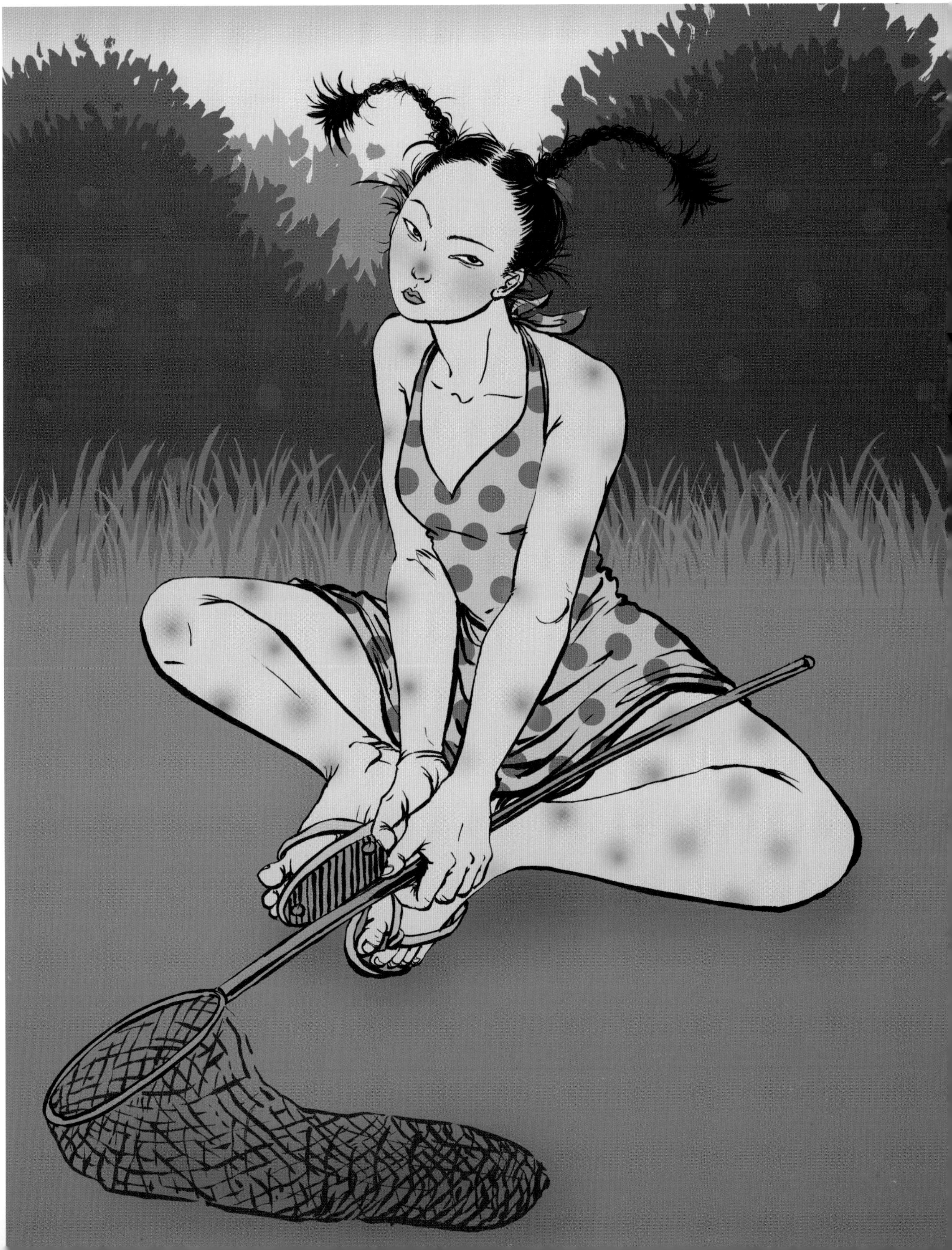

MOSCHITO 2002

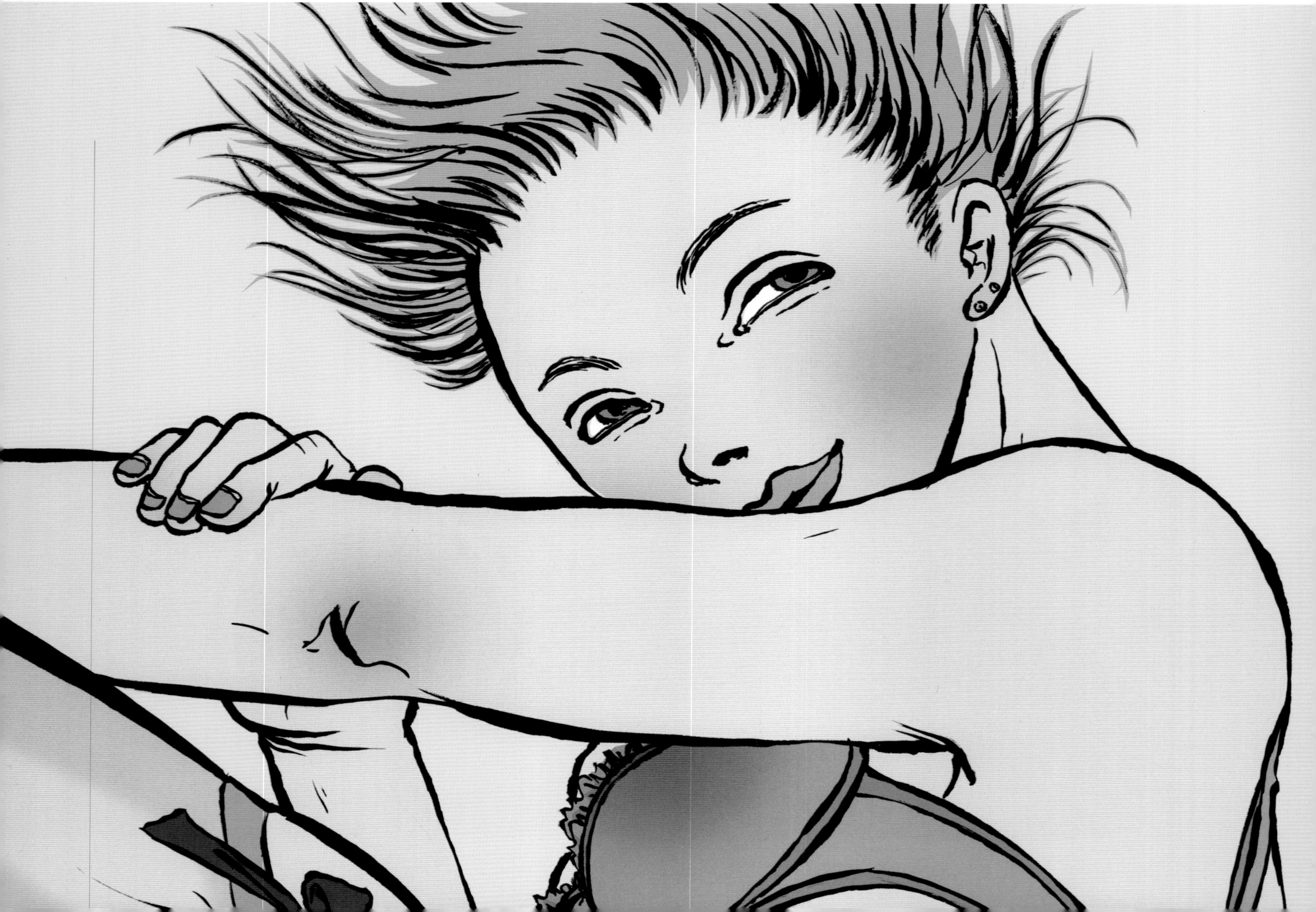

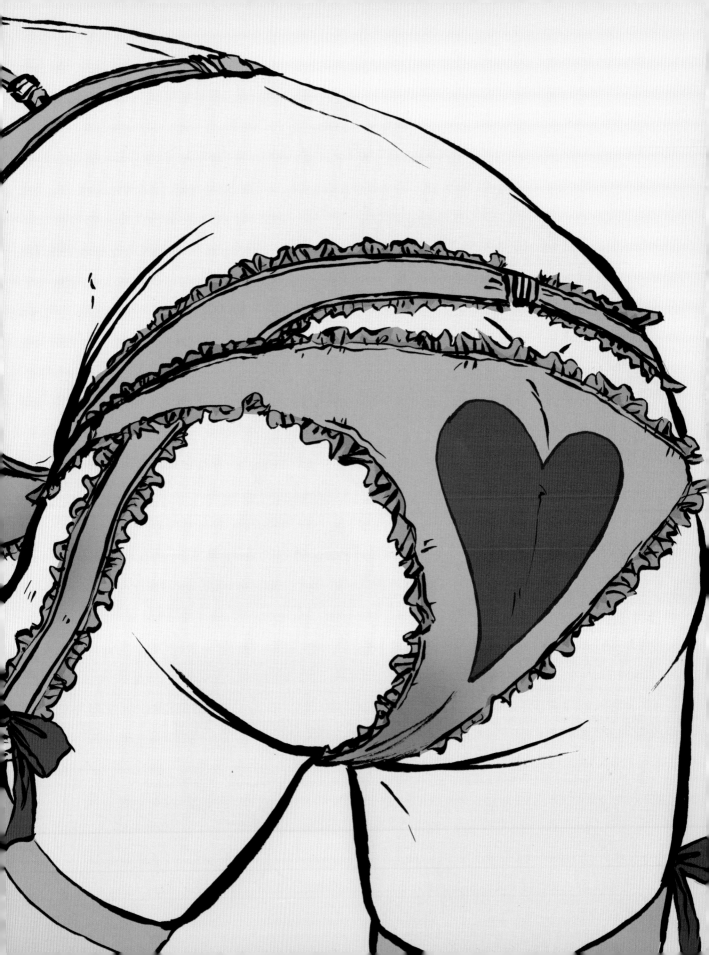

HiLDE RUBECKSEN

NORWAY
ROYAL COLLEGE OF ART, LONDON, UK
UNIVERSITY OF CENTRAL LANCASHIRE, UK

With almost childlike naïvety, Hilde's women are brought to life with a minimum of fuss, using simple ink-drawn figures scanned and later coloured on the computer. There is a sketchbook charm to these androgynous females, who are presented as empty outlined silhouettes, throwing the focus toward the highlighted garments. The quirkiness of Hilde's representational style exaggerates waist and hips and provides for large, expressive hands and fingers. Figures are dressed in body-conscious outfits that define their female shape with subtle charm and humour. Although the detail of the garment construction is kept to a minimum, each article of clothing is convincingly expressed on the page. These illustrations capture their subjects off-guard, sometimes with startled expressions. It is almost as if the women don't know why they have been singled out for special attention in this way.

LAURA McCAFFERTY

UK
NOTTINGHAM TRENT UNIVERSITY, UK

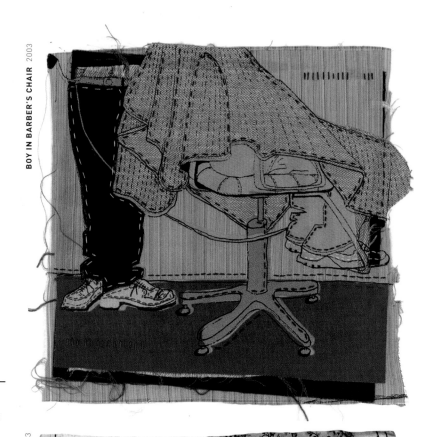

Using the unusual method of fabricated collage, Laura elaborates on everyday events such as going to the hairdresser or doing the grocery shopping. Laura spends weeks recording people and situations, their actions, conversations, clothing, and accessories. Working in Biro and acrylic paint for the original image, the finished line is then transferred onto silk-screen. Routine is vividly captured in floral patterns using appliqué, hand stitching, and paint. She usually works small, which gives the viewer the feeling that they are peeking in on a captured moment. Laura's fly-on-the-wall documentary style freeze-frames the moment with unsentimental realism. Each picture tells its own story in its assembly of fabric and stitched line. In her salon images she portrays real-life Cinderellas desperately wanting to go to the ball. The tools of the hairdresser's trade are carefully executed. The lotions are lined up with military precision. Her characters sit like royalty on their salon thrones while assistants conduct the ritual of transforming their lives with coiffures of predetermined style.

My fabric illustrations tell a personal story of the community around me. It is an individual view that combines craft skills with figurative imagery to create nostalgic pieces that document life today.

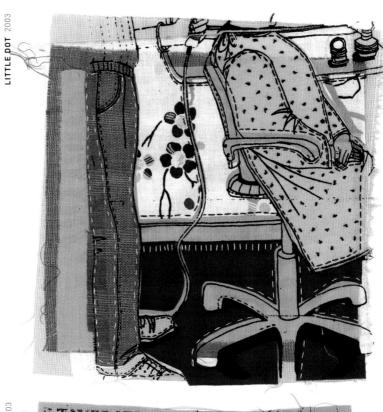

LITTLE DOT 2003

MARY WITH THE PINK TRAINERS 2003

laura mccafferty **47**

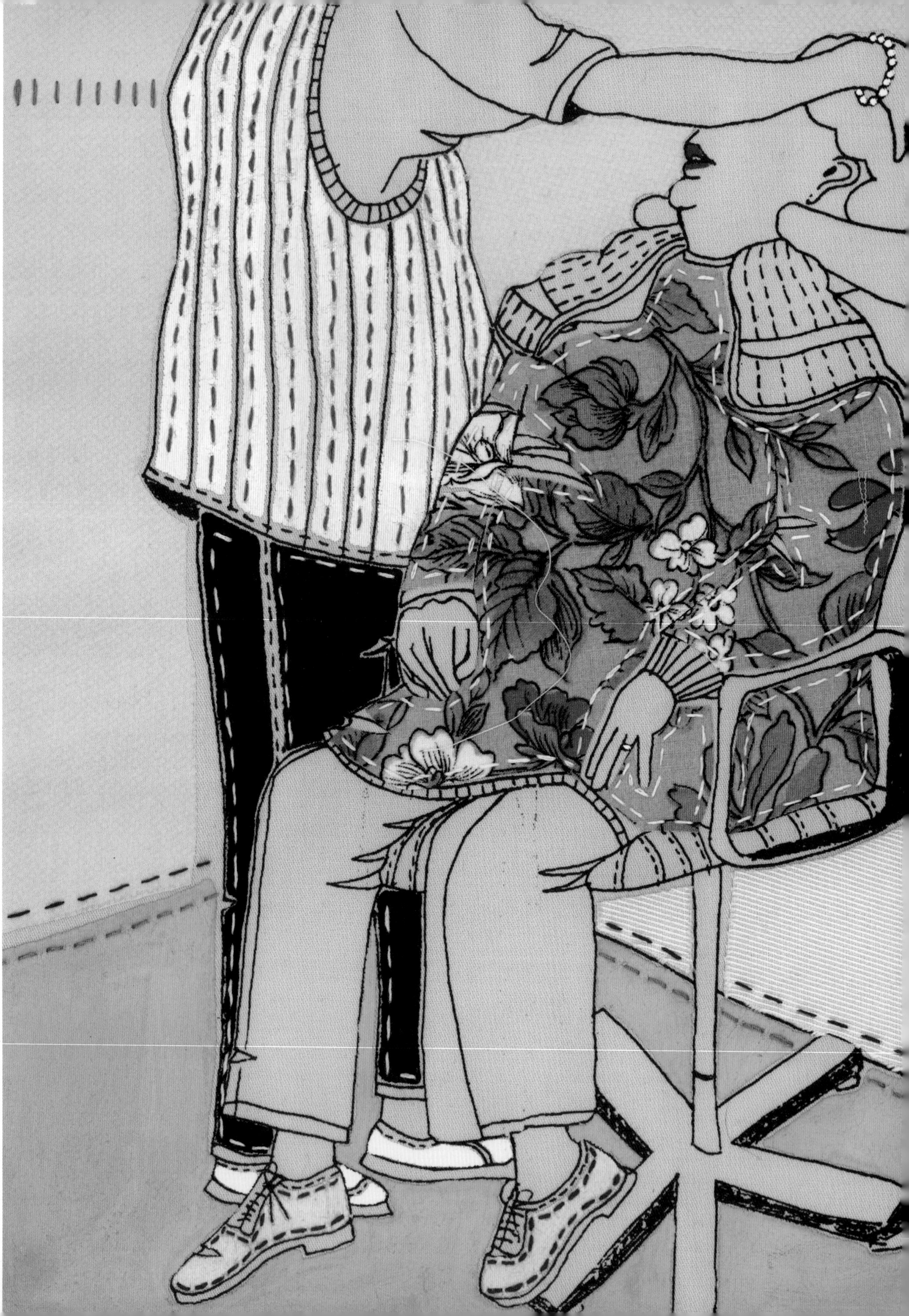

HAIR WASH 2003

With a strong focus on routine and appearance, I love to capture both quirkiness and formality in everyday fashion. It excites me how real people choose to visually express themselves — young or old.

LULU

GERMANY

KOLN INTERNATIONAL SCHOOL OF DESIGN, GERMANY

UNIVERSITAT DER KUNSTE, BERLIN, GERMANY

Lulu gains inspiration from her love of travelling and has collected a stack of old picture postcards from the 1950s and magazines from the 1960s. Sometimes she will sketch out ideas, and at other times she works directly on the computer. She uses all kinds of media, from pen and brush to Illustrator and Adobe Photoshop. Lulu's involvement with graphic animation is evident in her illustrations, which read more like film cells snipped from a movie reel. Her people obviously lead very busy lifestyles. They represent the city contingent who dash from one appointment to the next, snatching their lunch in order to check out the latest delivery of instore fashions. Predictably they move in circles that constantly demand an updated dress code. This is stylishly conveyed with orderly outlines filled with clean-cut applications of both colour and pattern.

I grew up in my parents' flower shop, with its colourful interior and lots of '70s people around me every day. I guess this is why I like to play with colours so much in my illustrations.

BUILD UP YOUR WARDROBE *INSTYLE* 2003

MARCOS CHIN

CANADA
ONTARIO COLLEGE OF ART AND DESIGN, TORONTO, CANADA

Marcos works by preparing pencil sketches which he scans and re-draws digitally, employing the sketch as a loose template. Consciously absorbing life around him (music, fashion, toys, animé) he relies upon his imagination to give him the freedom to develop his stylish illustrations. The use of colour is startling, consciously reigning-in a full palette in favour of striking tonal variations. His work has the appeal of a handpainted engraving or a Warhol print, articulated with an almost pop, psychedelic quality. The colour is always applied flat, employing a Manga-comic style to express both depth and shade. His characters have the self-assurance of the well heeled. Not for them the troubles of the daily grind. These people are out to enjoy themselves. Melissa stares out at us with the enigmatic poise and air of the sophisticate. Even at the pool, reduced to a minimal wardrobe, characters strut with a confidence that is out to get them noticed. The effervescence of the club scene (overleaf) is vividly captured by clever image manipulation and framing. The close-up face and reflected clubber in the spectacle lens are caught off-camera in an image that strains energetically at the confines of its frame.

MELISSA 2002

MARCOS

I remember when I was four years old my sister and I would play dress up. We used a towel for a skirt and my mother's handbag and jewellery as accessories. Then my sister put me into my mother's high-heeled shoes and walked me out into the hallway. I remember feeling excited and gorgeous and somewhat nervous at the same time; my sister glowed next to me. That was one of my earliest memories of how fun dressing up could be; that it was a means of exposing latent parts of myself. I felt different, more colourful, less of an introvert. For a moment, I was no longer that shy kid doodling in his story books.

STREET CRED

The clothes we wear often prove to be a more reliable barometer of ourselves than anything we may verbally explain. Although a cliché, it is true that our initial judgement of a person is based on how they appear. It is accepted that going against the norm can carry its own sense of style, yet you can no longer opt out by disregarding what you wear. In stating nothing, you are subconsciously saying something.

Today, the high street is a consumer jungle and the tribes within it continue to be increasingly conspicuous. With so much of today's global media preoccupied with visual language, clothing provides the ideal means to an understanding of self-expression and identity.

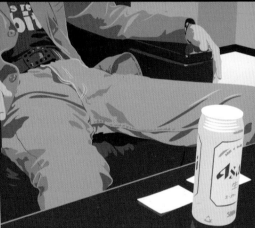

However, today's fashionable youth market seems disillusioned with the blatant consumerism that surrounds it. They have fashioned a uniform that is, more than ever, a direct response to their immediate lifestyle and requirements. There is far more of the feeling of comfort and convenience in youth couture than the traditional glamour of dressing up. This is not fashion just for fashion's sake – there is certainly no suffering for style in their "cool" approach.

In fact, there seems to be far more camouflage than overt display in current street fashion. As deliberately as mods and rockers stood out from

the crowd on Brighton beach, and punk's conspicuous anti-fashion drew attention to itself, today's street scene affords a fashion identity that nearly borders on the undetectable. Clothes shroud the wearer in a cloak of invisibility, with the added security of identifying the individual as part of a gang. In a society that is increasingly obsessed with surveillance, the obligatory hood and high collars act as protection and conceal the identity of the wearer. Clothes are beginning to mirror the fortification of the house or the protection of the car.

This has in no way resulted in mass uniformity. Creating a fashion identity has become a subtle art in its own right. Since there no longer exists a dictate on what is *de rigueur* each season, it relies upon the imagination and tastes of each tribe member to assemble a wardrobe that subtly projects their own personality and style.

Advancements in marketing and communication techniques have significantly enhanced the aesthetic understanding of fashion and the messages that can be communicated through clothes. The internet presents an ever-changing window on the world, documenting lifestyles and fashion in a previously undiscovered manner. Fascinating websites such as

www.japanesestreets.com have impressive levels of visitor traffic seeking out the hottest news on tribe culture and style.

The diversity of the fashion tribes out on the street continues to be as plentiful as the labels that previously promoted each new must-have brand. Still today, there remains the fact that certain garments will forever carry the cachet of an associated label and will linger beyond their expected sell-by date. Even if the reversed Stüssy baseball cap is (thankfully) a decreasing sight, most wardrobes will still contain a pair of Nike trainers or Levi jeans.

These streetwise counter customers continue to avert the camera's gaze away from the fashion runways and aim them toward these street catwalks. Even if the display is less overt, it still continues as an important litmus test on dress codes. The plethora of fashion styles that have evolved from their street roots have created a new perception of traditional dress, and one that is eagerly exploited by designers around the globe who are keen to be in touch with what is hip and cool.

In this section, illustrators from the USA and Canada; Australia and New Zealand; Germany, Spain, Sweden, and the UK expose the street styles within their own countries and continents.

For me, fashion has always been about creating your own individual style. Whether it be urban, punk, mod, or vintage, fashion allows us to wear our attitudes, interests, and lifestyle.

Daniel draws his inspiration from varied types of art forms – photography, fine art, movies, and music videos. Starting with a rough compositional sketch, Daniel will then work directly on the computer to produce his illustrations. His streetwise offspring are etched in a literal, observational style that befits his interpretation of the inoffensive youth culture around him. He employs a colour-by-numbers approach with a limited amount of fuss and embellishment. His illustrations are peopled with subjects in relaxed, everyday encounters with friends, carrying out the routines of daily life. These young people don't contend with the hang-ups of older generations. They are not aggressive with political agendas. They don't yet have the pressures of family life. They are dressed unpretentiously, blending into their own environment. This is a generation that doesn't stand out in the crowd – rather they constitute the crowd.

GIRL 2002

TREATS 2003

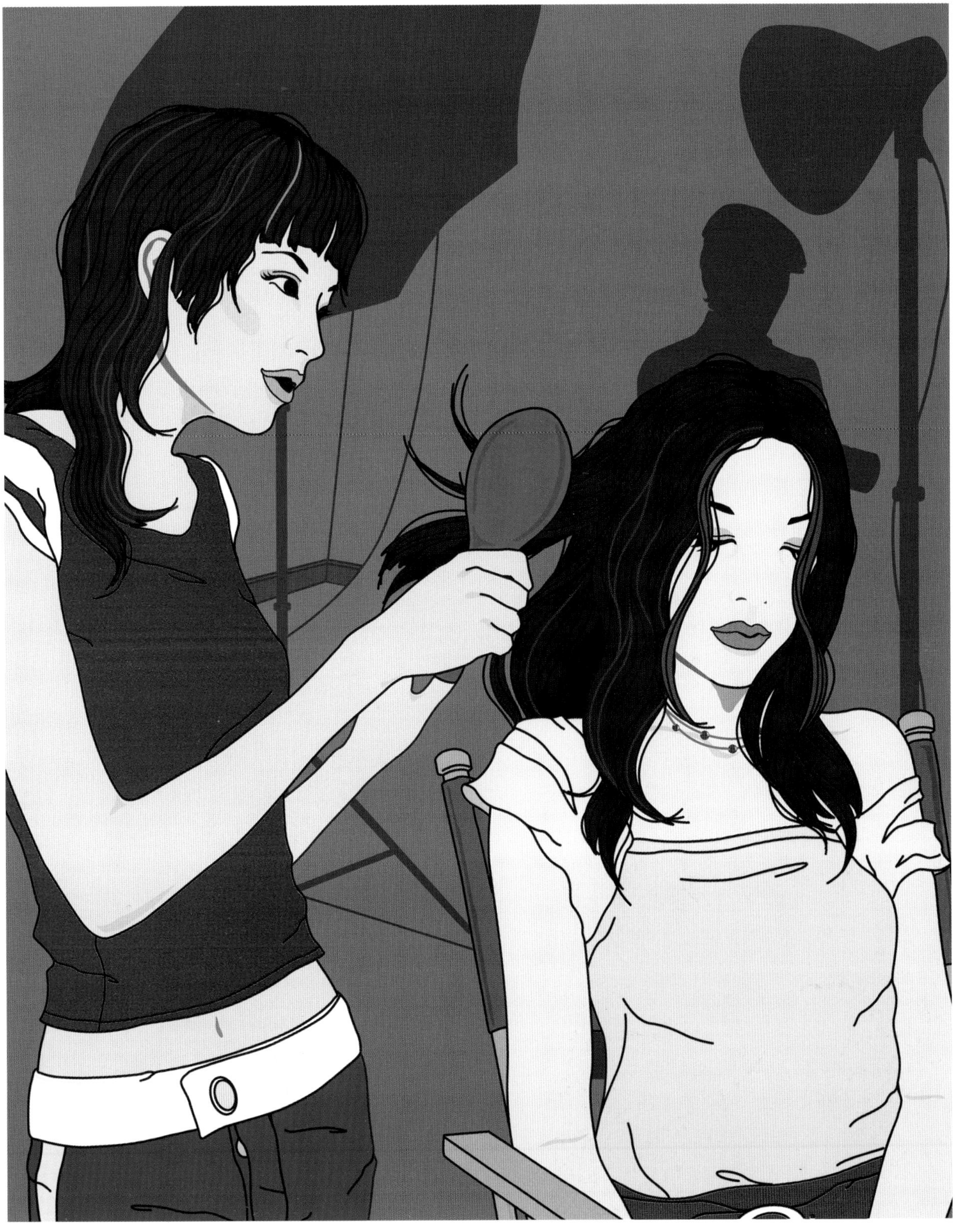

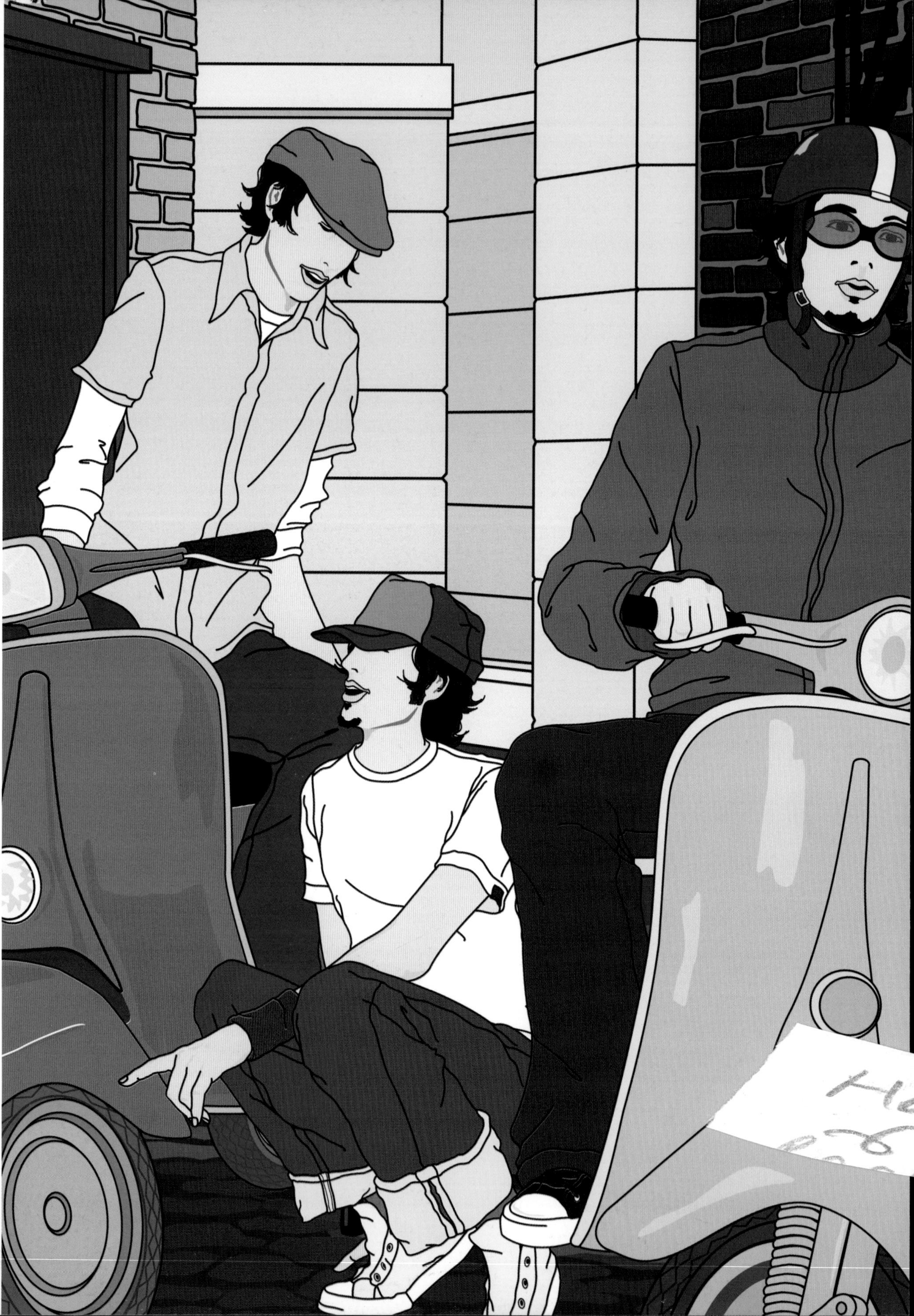

VESPAS 2002

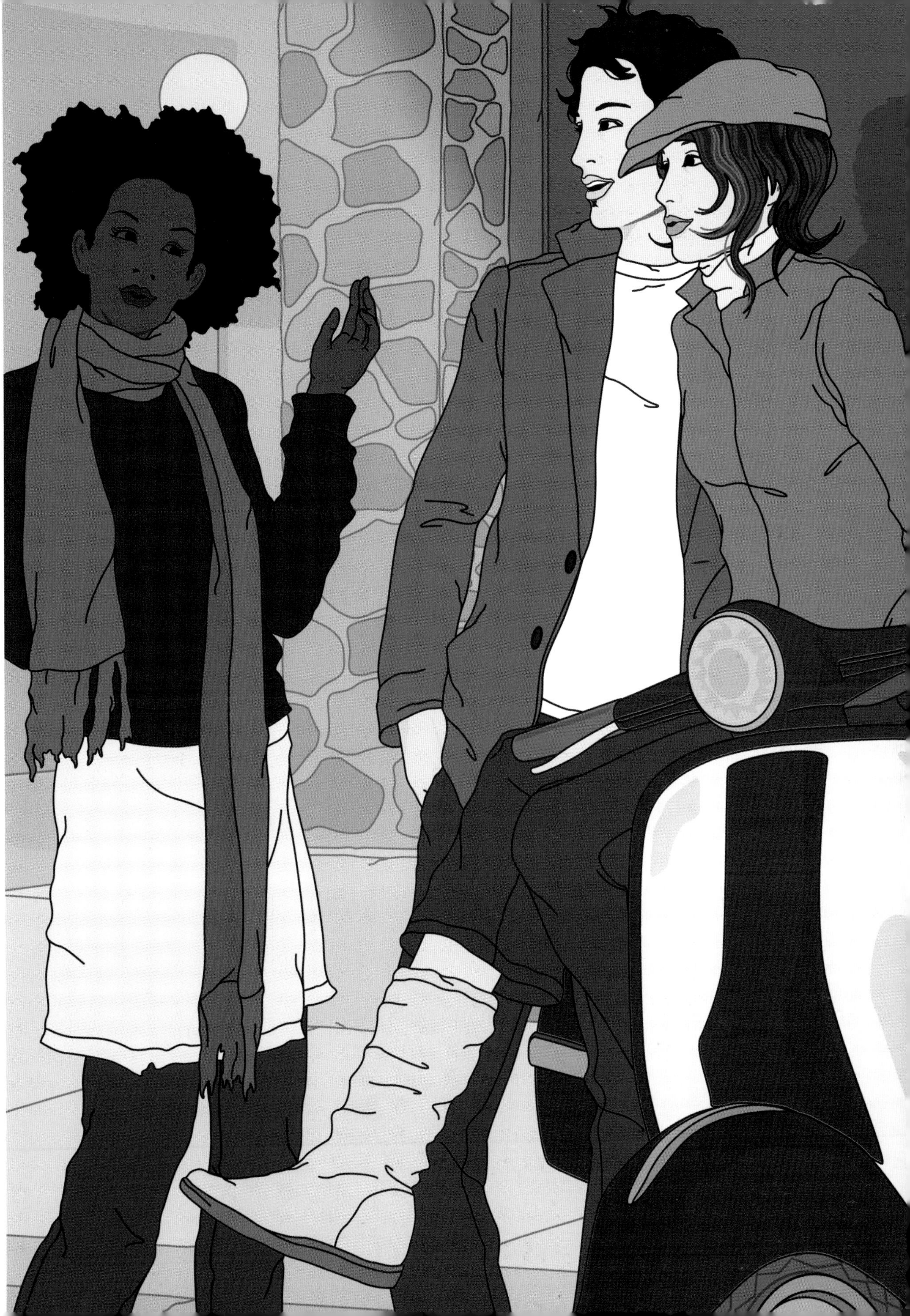

LAURA McLACHLAN

SPAIN
ESCUELA DE ARTE PAU GARGALLO, BARCELONA, SPAIN

Laura's depictions of contemporary fashion are reminiscent of the glossily styled photo shoots promoted by the latest lifestyle magazines. Her characters are skilfully framed within their environment by careful balancing and composition. Using a confident graphic style of representation, the effect is cleanly achieved by a combination of black ink, fibre pen, and watercolour. Prompted by photographic reference and source images that spark her imagination, this documentary style of mark-making provides Laura's illustrations with a suitably schematic precision. This style does not attempt to distort the event, but depicts an idealized scene within realistic surroundings.

FASHION AND ART: VERSACE MEETS WARHOL 2002

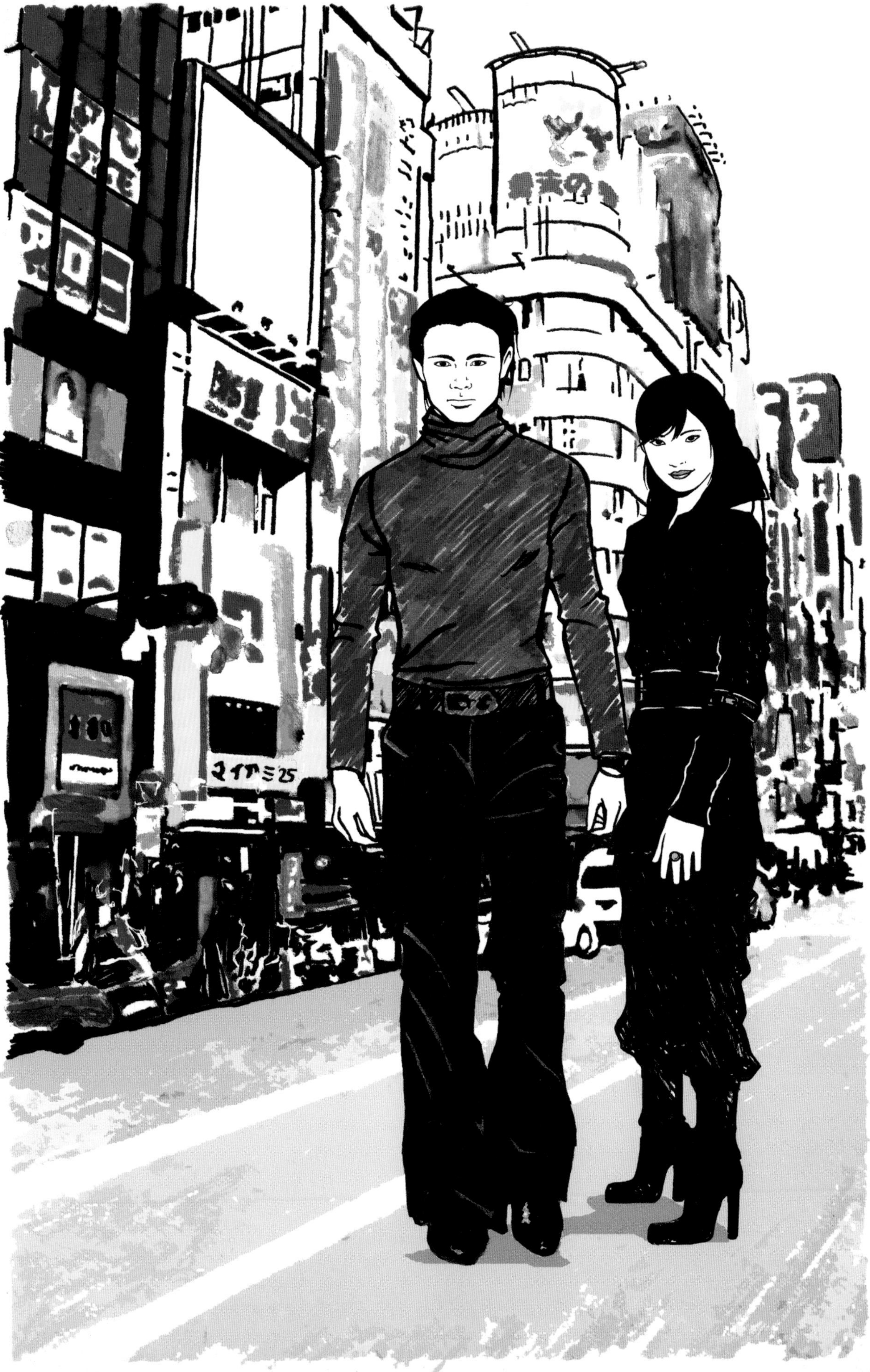
マイアミ25

Fashion illustration is a mode of expression that generates precise and rich descriptions of epochs as well as concrete moments, psychological states, lifestyles, and plastic trends.

CARMEN AMERICAN EAGLE OUTFITTERS 2003

BEN SHANNON

CANADA
SHERIDAN COLLEGE, OAKVILLE, ONTARIO, CANADA

Deriving his inspiration from the worlds of music and "sexy fashion," Ben prefers to draw directly on the computer screen working with Adobe Photoshop and Adobe Illustrator. Using dramatic optical angles to heighten the atmosphere of his scenes, Ben pulls the viewer into potent environments like a subjective film-maker. These drawings are full of heady atmosphere and driving energy. The stamping trainer sole is terrifically accentuated by the use of speed lines and graduated perspective. This has all the hallmarks and vibrancy of the best of DC Comic imagery. The strength of the image is articulated in bold strokes of line and colour. With a minimum of information, Ben captures the pose effortlessly. The offset aerial view of the dancer is cleverly framed within the composition, heightened by her arms punching out to the rhythm of the dance.

A vice for some, entertainment for others, fashion is the advertising we wear to tell others about who we are. Friendship forming, romance enhancing, and wink inducing. Enjoyed by just about everyone...

JOSIE LOUISE

UK

SURREY INSTITUTE OF ART AND DESIGN, UK
UNIVERSITY COLLEGE, LONDON, UK

A graduate in fashion promotion and illustration, Josie adopts a merchandising eye in her clever depiction of passing market trends. Her confident marker-pen delineation, in combination with thick acrylic paint, sometimes applied over a background of torn tissue paper or newsprint, brings these characters to life in a frank and articulate manner. All her personalities are easily recognizable from real life. They are archetypal teenage girls from down the road who attempt to imitate the latest teen magazine style. They watch us from the page with large questioning eyes like stylish derivatives of Wyndham's *The Midwich Cuckoos*. The image Urban Princess, (overleaf) with its smudges of newsprint and fragmented song lyric text (from *6 Underground* by Sneaker Pimps) bears a similarity to the collages of Kurt Schwitters.

DKNY 2003

MIU MIU AND Y3 2003

I love the stylish illustrations, album covers, and adverts of the 1940s and '50s. I also find great inspiration in contemporary culture, including cartoons, comics, music videos, and the internet. My images tend to reflect trend and lifestyle rather than focusing on gender or physical dimensions. The message in my work is that fashion can be inspiring, vibrant, and energetic.

MARC JACOBS 2003

VERSUS 2003

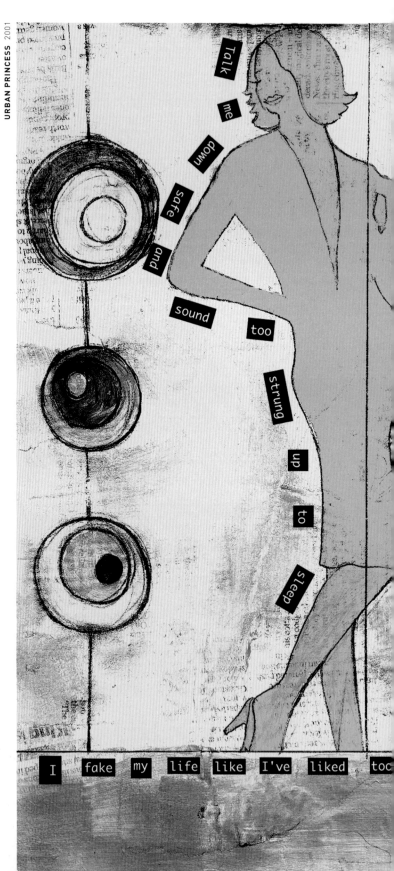

Talk me down safe and sound too strung up to sleep

I fake my life like I've liked too

ANTHONY KOLBER

AUSTRALIA
SWINBURNE NATIONAL SCHOOL OF DESIGN
MELBOURNE, AUSTRALIA

Anthony conjures up his striking illustrations working primarily with Adobe Illustrator and Macromedia Freehand. He directs his original inspiration toward a distorted and imaginative conclusion, developed via a mix of hand-drawn and photo-based reference. The use of boldly blocked-out colour secures an atmosphere redolent of a 1960s' Warhol screenprint. This mechanistic approach to depicting his characters leaves the viewer on the outside looking in. Stimulated by both fashion and hip-hop, Anthony reinterprets this imagery in a recognizable personal style. This is not a society that you can join unless you have the same dress code. It is a closed group. Often faces are incomplete so that their identity is preserved. Hoods cover heads in the coded mask of individuality.

As I have been illustrating for some years now, I find that my subject matter has begun shifting from the commonplace and standard to themes that contain a lot more abstraction. I now try to express individuals and characters in a less figurative sense and in a more idealistic context.

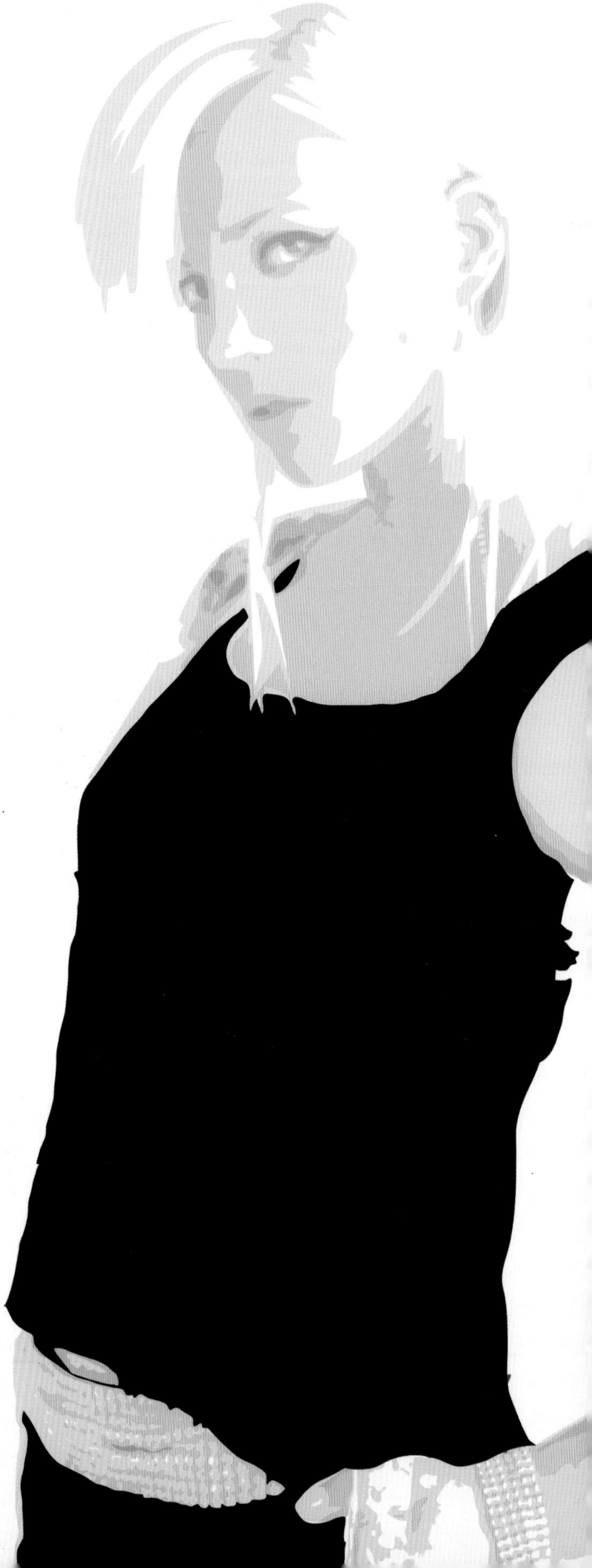

DAVID PFENDLER

USA

PARSONS SCHOOL OF DESIGN, NEW YORK, USA

Working almost exclusively with digital media (mainly Adobe Photoshop and Illustrator) there still remains the underlying appeal of freehand execution in much of David's illustrations. Sometimes he will create rough sketches directly onto the computer using a Wacom digital pad. He considers that the computer allows him to keep all the options open and keeps the work both fresh and dynamic. David's narratives are placed within the easy-going lifestyle of Sunday lie-ins and casual street diversions, with his figures beautifully framed within each well-balanced composition. Rarely exploiting anything other than a monochromatic muted colour palette, each illustration is contained within the subtle use of dynamics and contrasts. The application of clean, flat colour as an indication of light and shade is cleverly managed, providing enough information to add volume and weight to each illustration.

I like to think of my work as urban lifestyle imagery with a fashion bent. Fashion has become so cultural. The urban influence along with the "musicality" of style has changed the way we relate to our environment and how we present ourselves to the world. How all of this is represented continues to evolve along with changing tastes and expressions.

david pfendler **77**

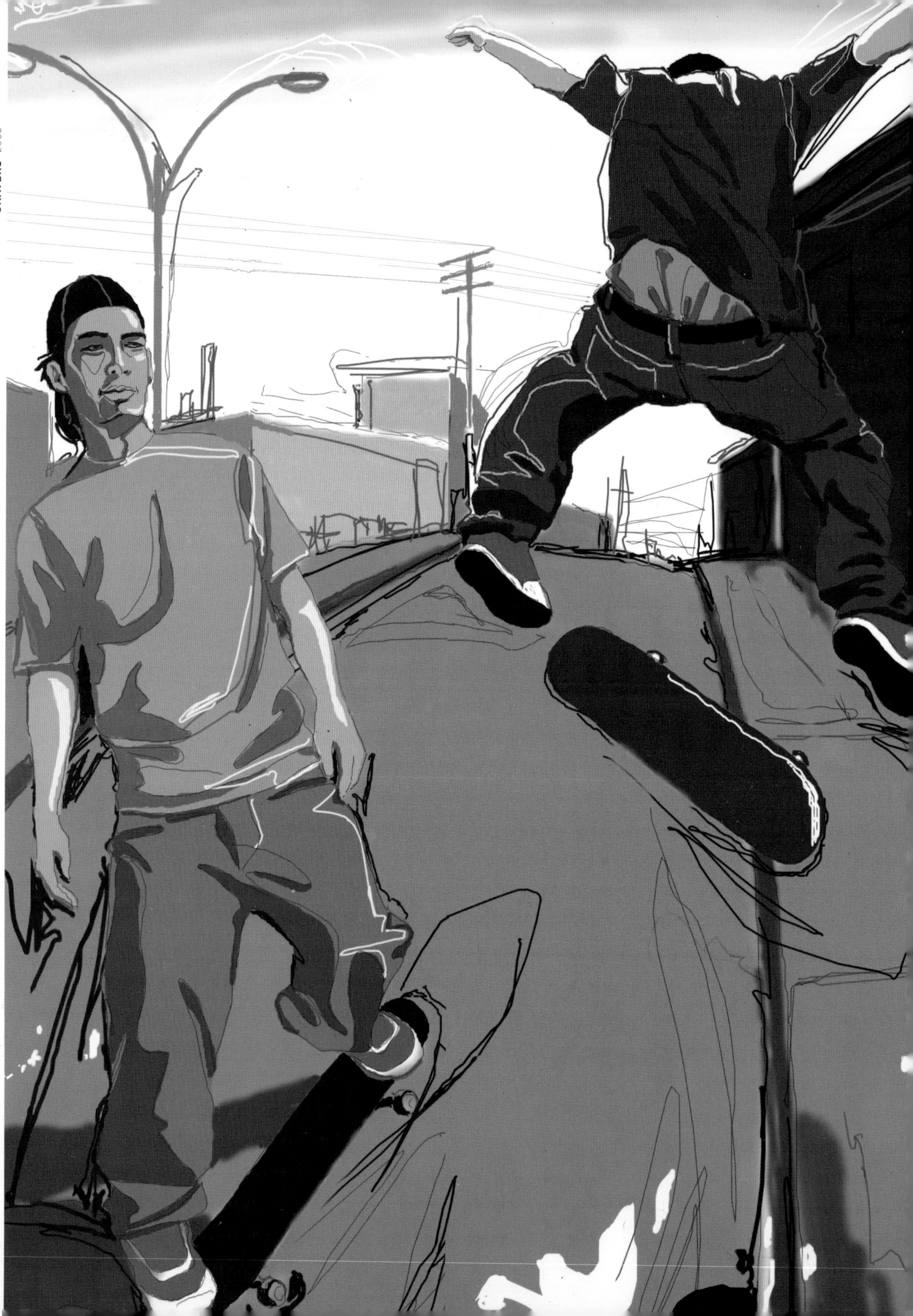

ALANNA CAVANAGH

CANADA
UNIVERSITY OF TORONTO, CANADA

Alanna sketches with a lively line that articulates her characters in a pleasingly loose treatment. Her figures are depicted with the simplest of added colour or texture. No superfluous information is allowed to clutter or invade the page. This becomes almost a shorthand form of graphic depiction. Working from an eclectic mix of source material, Alanna documents her findings with an amusing reflection on present styles and trends: a teenage youth, headphones blocking out his environment; a grin-and-bear-it victim of the "healthy mind-healthy body" brigade; and the sexy shopper who confidently swings her carrier bags as she sashays along the sidewalk.

My illustration style has been described as humorous, bold, and squiggly! I draw inspiration from many sources, including flea markets, design magazines, textiles, and clothing. Objects discovered one day – such as a wire birdcage, vintage jacket, or a dress mannequin – often appear in my illustration the next!

YOGA WOMAN 2003

Breathe Deeply

WHACK 2003

This Song is So whack.

MONICA HELLSTROM

SWEDEN

BECKMANS DESIGNHOGSKOLA, STOCKHOLM, SWEDEN

Monica employs a fluid representational style that articulates her smart people with a minimum of information. She doodles a lot to plan out her images, which can be inspired by anything from people on the subway, to her dreams. Her technique suggests the paintings of Raoul Dufy, with its simple representational style and use of colour. She does not like the current vogue for streamlining already existing images, and will either sketch out initial ideas on paper to later scan into the computer, or draw directly on the computer using a Wacom pad. Monica's style can range from edgy to commercial, from arty to eager-to-please. Her palette is often made up of intensely contrasting colours that emphasize the scene. Although there is a falsification and caricature to most of her figures, this does not block their warmth and charm to the viewer. These are essentially happy and contented people. Looking out at us with their quizzical gaze, they invite us to come on in, because the water's fine. They represent a lifestyle that is secure and unthreatening. Auburn-haired Lynn (overleaf) clearly inhabits a stress-free world where walking the dog or curling up in front of the fireplace are the only demands on her time.

ST JOHN *BIG* MAGAZINE 2003

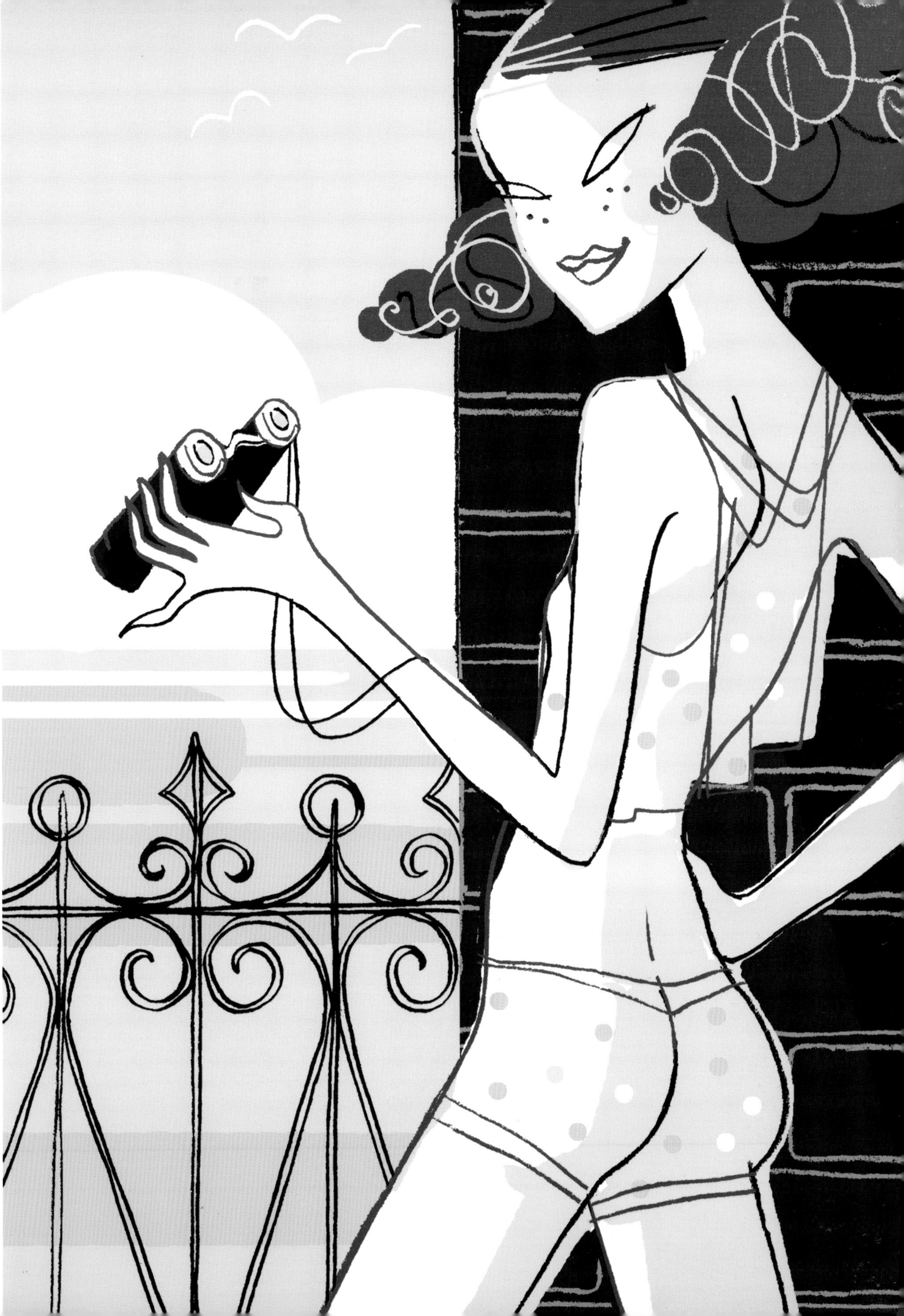

I want to separate beauty and fashion. Youth today are too involved with beauty rather than fashion. It's all about wearing the right brands, not about wearing something interesting. All it takes is money. I miss the experimental playfulness of the 1980s, when looking cool was much more important than looking good. Another thing I would welcome back is women, as opposed to girls. Girls are so unglamorous, they have no experience of life, they're not dangerous or interesting.

LYNN IN THE CITY/LYNN AT THE FIREPLACE *FASHION MAGAZINE* 2002

FIONA MACLEAN

NEW ZEALAND

AUCKLAND TECHNICAL INSTITUTE, NEW ZEALAND

ART AND TECHNOLOGY OF MAKE-UP COLLEGE
SYDNEY, AUSTRALIA

URBAN LOVE 2003

Mixing the traditional media of gouache, pastel, and pen with digital media, Fiona packages her depictions of youth in easily identifiable street scenes. Often using a digital camera to capture this vibrant environment, Fiona pulls in inspiration from a mixture of contemporary popular art and culture. Always working from initial sketches, these are scanned and drawn up using Adobe Illustrator to trace the outline. The handsome couple stride side-by-side against a chalk line cityscape, their contrasting black and white outfits expressed with a simple flooding of silhouette against the single expanse of background colour. A vibrant heart-shaped handbag seems to confirm their relationship. The blue-haired fashion victim is exhausted by a day's shopping. Consumerism surrounds her in the form of adverts and shopping bags.

Fashion is a reflection of what is going on within contemporary culture; with music, film, technology, visual arts, architecture, photography, and street cultures all feeding off each other. Fashion is as definitive of a certain period in time and as important as art. It's a chameleon, always changing and forever elusive. Fashion gives youth a form of self-expression, the ability to rebel, to stand out in the crowd or be accepted into a selective group. I try to create strong, capable, and extremely feminine women. It all tells a story – the hair, the makeup, the clothes!

CHANEL JUNKIE 2001

MELANCHOLIA 2002

SEAN MACFARLANE

UK

UNIVERSITY OF BRIGHTON, UK
SOUTHAMPTON INSTITUTE, UK
EPSOM SCHOOL OF ART AND DESIGN, UK

In an almost Dadaist application of photo-montage technique, Sean challenges convention with a very personal spin on contemporary style. He enjoys reinterpreting found material and his working process begins very traditionally with scissors and paste. Cuttings of faces, body parts, clothing, and accessories are reshaped and reconstructed, making them change in appearance and feeling even before their development at the digital stage of work. His disquieting assemblies of facial contours seem to proffer a cynical appraisal of the fashion scene's constant marketing of traditionally accepted beauty. Once happy with the scanned composition, the image goes through the final (and longest) stage of development with the manipulation of colour, contrast, and texture via countless image adjustments and filtering in Adobe Photoshop. This surreal digitally-constructed work challenges accepted views by assembling images that force the viewer to re-evaluate their opinions. The chaotic beginnings of the images are tamed with a strong direction of composition and style.

I enjoy the idea of stealing a look or idea away from its real-life environment and reconstituting it in a new context. My figures often look lost and confused, as if they have been woken up in a world that looks the same, but feels somehow different, as if from a dream.

SMILEY BANANA 2002

HAT MAN IN HAWAII 2003

ORIENTAL FLOWER 2002

GYPSY BLUE 2003

LUC LATULIPPE

CANADA
SHERIDAN COLLEGE, OAKVILLE, ONTARIO, CANADA

Luc produces his humorous and appealing vector art entirely on a Macintosh. Always working from initial sketches, these are scanned into Adobe Photoshop, then placed into an Adobe Illustrator document and traced from there using a Wacom tablet. These clearly etched characters don't seem to be too far away from the latest TV sitcom. The teenage fashion victims, travelling home with their conspicuously designer-labelled carrier bags, effortlessly come alive on the page. They are cleverly characterized with a detailed dress code that stretches all the way from their heads to their toes. This condensing of image into simple, stylish comic invention and line has an extensive cartoon history – comic books are an admitted source of inspiration – and is again economically achieved in the sale-hunters' contented glances as they contemplate their latest bargains. Luc often borders his images in interesting rhythmic shapes. There is a dreamlike cloud suggestion to his delineation around the shopping couple, and the horoscope representations are framed like a series of collectable pin badges.

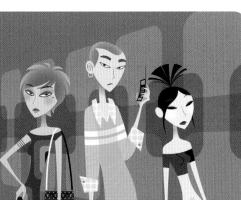

I find that cultures around the world are being hijacked, watered-down and censored, homogenized and re-packaged, and sold back to us. I don't look anything like the people in my drawings. I avoid big malls and the fancy clothes shopping areas. I buy my clothes from thrift shops, and even comic-book stores.

luc latulippe **91**

ARTHUR MOUNT

USA
CALIFORNIA COLLEGE OF THE ARTS, USA

Created with a revitalizing clarity of technique
and resourcefulness, Arthur's illustrations
are peopled with young sophisticates in a
clear, no-nonsense style of execution. His
is a cleaned-up vision of the scene out on
the streets. There is no offensive graffiti or
unpleasant disorder to these lifestyles.
By using flat blocks of shade and tone,
this seemingly healthy existence is further
amplified in the unblemished skin and freshly
laundered clothes of the characters. The
framing of each realistic figure on the page
is naturally established with a stylist's eye for
arrangement and balance.

I'd welcome the increased use of illustration for
magazine editorial fashion spreads, and judging
by the quantity of email I receive from readers
regarding my illustrations, I don't think I'm alone.

PRADA *OUT* MAGAZINE 2003

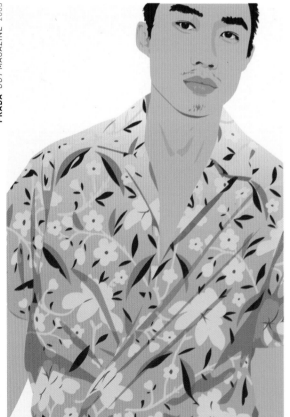

MICHAEL KORS *OUT* MAGAZINE 2003

L'OREAL 2003

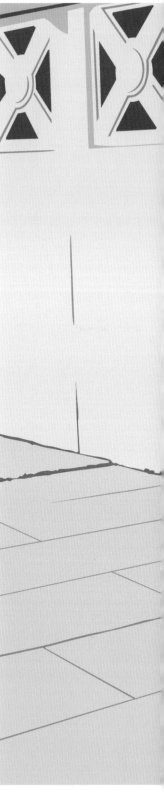

PINK BIKINI 2002

LAURA-JULIE GRIESCH

GERMANY
LETTE-VEREIN, BERLIN, GERMANY

Using bold, economical mark-making, Laura-Julie has a representational style that accurately evokes the moods and characters she is describing. This simplification of the image is skilfully achieved in the sketch of the satchel-carrying youth whose face and hands are not drawn, but are implied by the deft employment of colour and pose. The potent atmosphere of the hung-over friends, crashed-out in front of the TV (overleaf) is achieved with the minimum of extraneous information. We can interpret the characters simply through their identifiable trainers and knitted caps. The silhouetted forms of the figures, reduced to simply blocked black profiles, intensifies their anonymity. Laura-Julie's work is similar to the style perfected in the 1940s and '50s by the French fashion illustrator René Gruau, who represented everything through suggestion and arrangement.

I like to delve in and out of every
definition of culture I experience. Past,
present, and my own future fantasies are
fuelled by the excitement of what goes on
around me. What's contemporary now
may be forgotten tomorrow.

STYLE COUNCIL

Style has inevitably become a personal issue. Escalating pressure in our information-led society press-gangs us into communication at all costs. The man-made environment that surrounds us only serves to underline the importance of lifestyle trends and designer brands in any expression of personal style.

Style gurus seem to lie in wait around every corner. However, we no longer rely on received pearls of wisdom to instruct the way we view and express ourselves. Fashion editors like Anna Wintour may continue to advise over hemline lengths but they are no longer essential to steer us in the right direction. People seem increasingly prepared to challenge these mantras and to make their own personal style decisions.

This new-found confidence in making individual choice about self-image was nurtured in the latter part of the 20th century and now almost everyone has enough knowledge to be a fully paid-up member of the "style council."

This is not just restricted to the clothes we wear. The manner in which we decorate and furnish our homes; the way we cook and serve our food; the modes of behaviour that we invent

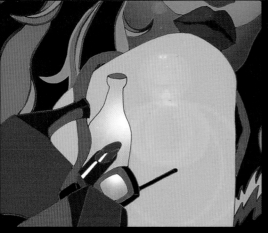

for the most routine of activities; all of these are projections of an image and style that we wish to be associated with. Fashion designers have been quick to take up on this development. Pioneered by the entrepreneurism of Ralph Lauren and Calvin Klein and the lure of global licensing, many designers now have their own household and lifestyle ranges.

However, being part of the "style council" hasn't always proved easy. In 1947, with postwar rationing still in place, the excesses of the 20m (22yd) of fabric used by Christian Dior in just one "New Look" skirt was beyond the reach of all but the most affluent of women. Other styles that were equally provocative – because they were unattainable – were Mary Quant's mini-skirt revolution in the 1960s, the punk excesses of Vivienne Westwood in the 1980s and, in the same decade, the expensive glamour of Versace and Lagerfeld, which was, to top it all, promoted by flawless supermodels.

In total contrast to the emergence of the supermodel in the 1980s, came the birth of alternative magazines such as *i-D* and *The Face*. These magazines paved the way for today's

fashion journals, in their revelation that fashion need not be all brand names and exclusivity. In a society that was already drenched in visualization, they documented new style identities that were being created by real people. Terry Jones aimed the cameras of *i-D* magazine and caught contemporary lifestyle head-on in the street in a way that rejoiced in the individual and unique fashion to be found there. He delighted in acknowledging that this was an age of self-design that was available to everyone.

Individuality has now become the by-word in today's fashionable market place. The source of reference is far wider than what the shelves of fashion stores have to offer. Style aficionados are not just familiar with the catwalks of Paris and Milan, but are fully aware of exactly what clothes Kylie is sporting in her latest music video. What once remained restricted to the rarified hands of a master couturier has now been usurped by today's wannabes who progressively fashion their own unique look and distinctive wardrobes.

The work of the illustrators featured in this section is convincing testament to the notion that everyone can be their own creator of style.

DANIEL EGNEUS

SWEDEN

Although Daniel has no formal training, his illustrations are made with the sophisticated technique of a tried-and-tested craftsman. In an approach that merges the simplicity and minimalism of a DC Comic with the cultured and refined mannerism of Egon Schiele, Daniel skilfully projects attitude and style onto his figures. Beginning with a quantity of preparatory sketches, he preserves the spontaneity of his mark-making by immediately painting onto the roughs. He uses a wide variety of traditional media (acrylics, oil, crayons, pencil, ink, and watercolour) as well as enhancing his originals with filter work on the computer. The upward stretch of the leopardprint female zigzags across the page, the sequence of her contorted body is beautifully stylized and delineated. The channel-hopping brunette is clearly a classy individual resembling a 1950s' existentialist. She is presented cross-footed without any surplus delineation on her garments. The arrangement is almost insect-like and deftly achieved.

LEOPARDSPOTS 2003

ILLY 2003

Sometimes I just draw everything without the help of the computer: it's not like I'm
following a structure when I draw, I just do the things that seem to be working at
that particular moment. In my pictures, I seldom try to convey a certain message.
Instead, I see them as the mere registration of my everyday impressions, in
particular those of my friends and the things we do.

SATOSHI MATSUZAWA

JAPAN
AOYAMA GAKUIN UNIVERSITY, TOKYO, JAPAN

The effectiveness of Satoshi's work is in the simplicity and clarity that he brings to his powerful illustrations. These are wonderfully descriptive depictions of an idealized society of females who relax and pose like preening animals. There are definite Art Nouveau overtones in these representations, with their broad undulating lines and sweeping body contours. These women have identifiable ancestors in the distinctive poster art of Alphonse Mucha. The portrait opposite is suffused with the heady aroma of Barbara Hulanicki's 1970s' Biba aesthetic. The ingenious use of simple geometrics to express the dress and flamboyant hat in the image below are achieved with the clarity of a medieval woodcut. Overleaf, a gracefully drawn figure reclines across the page in a sinuous surging line, her cascading hair a river of solid black.

Thinking about fashion, I am conscious that poses, styles, and situations are as important as clothes. I like 1960s and '70s women's fashion — it is very cute, sexy, and groovy. I like to imagine transforming my illustrations into movie scenes.

NATASCHA ENGLEMANN

USA/GERMANY

FREIE KUNSTAKADEMIE, DUSSELDORF, GERMANY

HEINRICH-HEINE UNIVERSITAT, DUSSELDORF, GERMANY

FREIE UNIVERSITAT, BERLIN, GERMANY

Having painted since childhood, Natascha studied photography and video at university. This gave her the opportunity to explore animation and eventually to develop her own unique style and idiom through 2-D illustration. She believes that the message contained in an illustration should be comprehensible at a glance. Her initial rough sketches are achieved using a blend of pencil, markers, acrylic, and watercolour techniques, and are then translated using Adobe Photoshop, Illustrator, and Freehand. Natascha refers to these illustrations as emotional landscapes. There is a trance-like condition to these images: the figures are like illusions drifting within each frame, fused or emerging from the vaporous backgrounds. The flower-bearing male is statuesque in his captured stance. Colour is applied delicately, and then heightened with an acute accent of contrasting colour. Patterns are overlayed to accentuate the design of a fabric. As in a dream, some things in Natascha's images register with defined clarity while others remain a blurred memory.

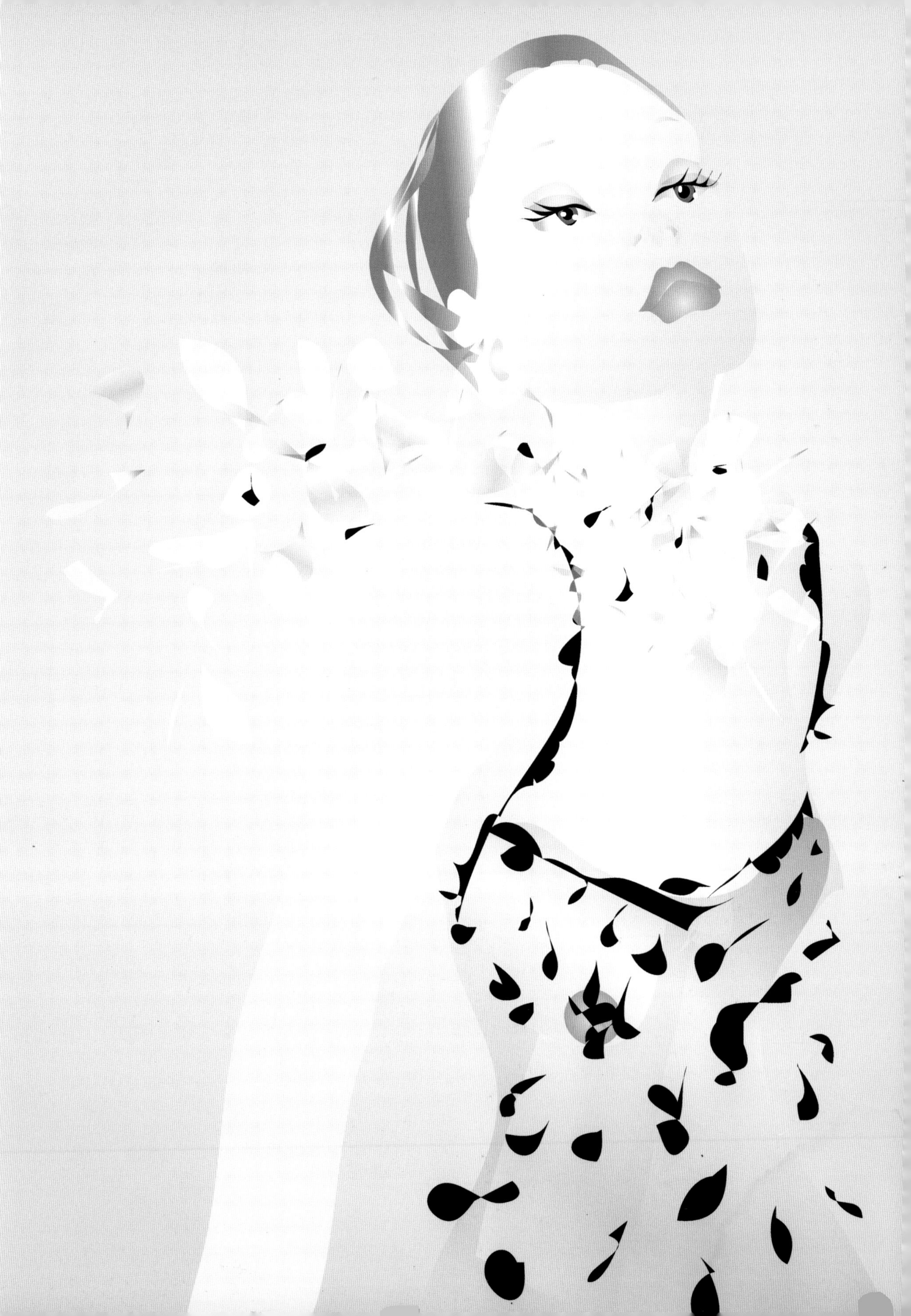

BLOND GIRL 2003

I work intuitively, and each illustration is a challenge, meaning that every single picture I finish has its own emotional colouring. There is never a "no-go" in the expression of the figures or things I create. The more expressive they are, the more I formalize the whole composition.

CLAIRE ANDERSON

UK

GLASGOW SCHOOL OF ART, SCOTLAND
UNIVERSITY OF GLASGOW, SCOTLAND

An über-feminine narrative runs throughout my work — these doyens of style live to shop. Each illustration is embroidered, a traditionally female craft; linear stitch brings them to life.

Despite having studied textile design, Claire's work has become pointedly more illustrative and graphic rather than slavishly following a traditional textile appearance. She begins with a pencil sketch and then uses this image as a guide to free-stitch the drawing itself. Claire usually works on a heavy cotton or canvas – the fabric becoming her piece of paper. Using a sewing machine, Claire carefully crafts her characters with all the fluid expression of a sketch. These free-hand embroidered drawings are as confidently created as if she was sketching onto the page. Claire has used this technique in a range of scales, from small vignettes to large murals. Advertising imagery and fashion photography from magazines are her main sources of inspiration. Claire's observations on fashion have the wit of a satirical cartoon – she endows her dogs with more character than her faceless figures. These pets feature throughout her work in an acknowledgment of the extra style points that the addition of a manicured poodle or coated miniature dog can add.

ANYA 2003

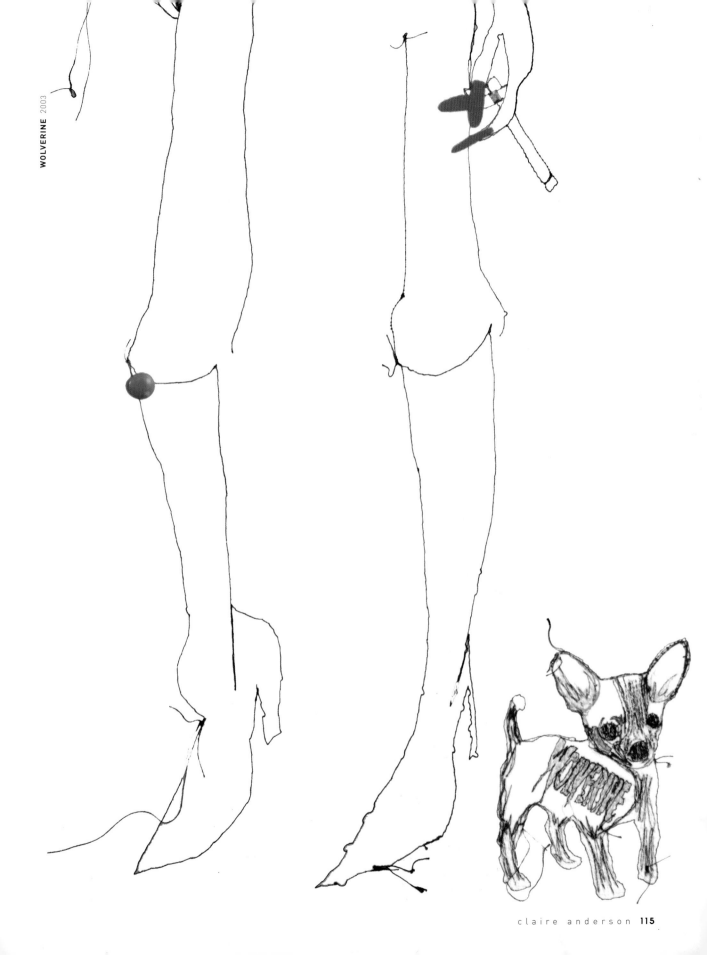

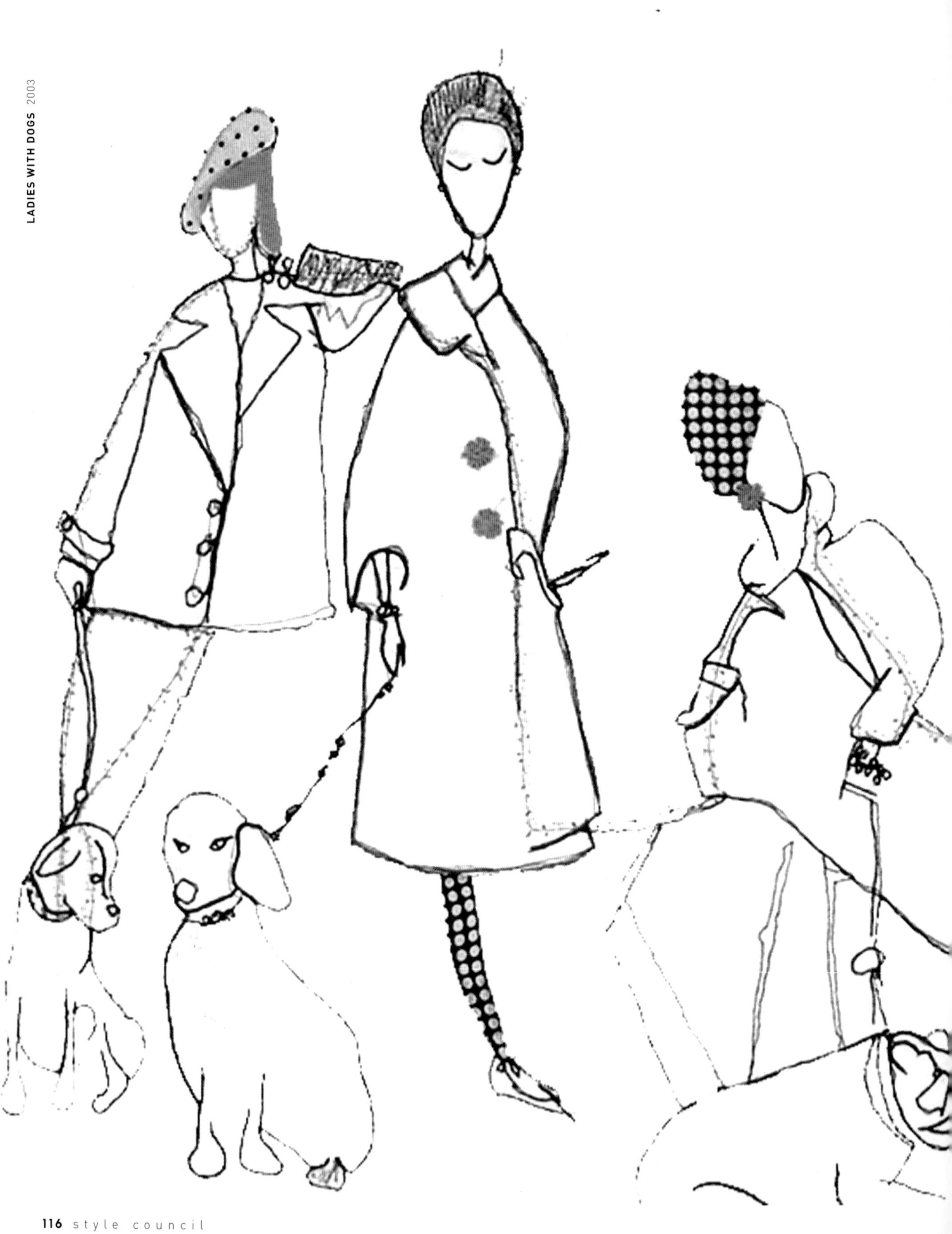

PINGLET

SINGAPORE
CURTIN UNIVERSITY OF TECHNOLOGY, PERTH, AUSTRALIA

Using her own rich imagination, Pinglet draws directly onto the computer, taking advantage of the full potential of the vector-driven software of Adobe Illustrator and Freehand. Her doe-eyed girls are blocked out in confident colours and rely on a minimum of detail. There is a sinewy rhythm to the contours and shapes that cleverly circumnavigate each composition. The personality of each character is economically depicted. Pinglet's females flaunt the coy innocence of Betty Boop with their wide-faced, doll-like appearance. In the picture opposite, the restriction of the full face with its single kohl-etched and elongated eye imparts the impression of an ancient Egyptian wall-painting. The waves of blushing pink lines in the Veronica Lake look-a-like overleaf has all the impact and confidence of a René Gruau advertisement. Figures are framed in each picture with a skilled visual balance.

ZOUKETTE 2002

It all started in kindergarten – I used to paint flowers and animals on my classmates. Being born in the 1970s probably skewed my tastes toward that era; Rudi Gernreich and Mary Quant are my fashion heroes. I live vicariously through my girls; they wear stuff that I wish I could wear, they're my alter egos.

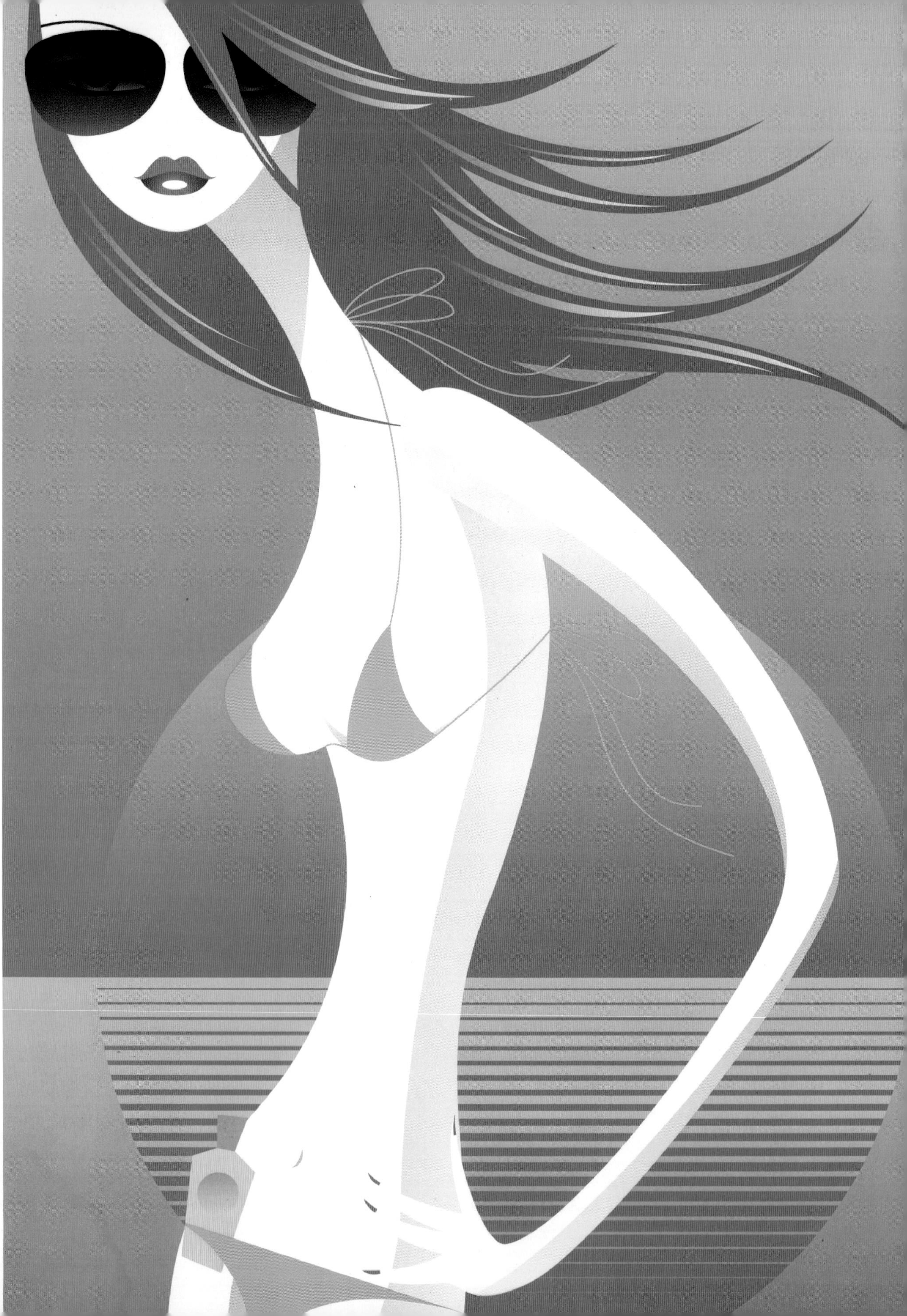

SOLAR 2002

TUESDAY MOURNING

USA

BRIGHAM YOUNG UNIVERSITY, SALT LAKE CITY, USA

A very personal interpretation of the human figure endows Tuesday's characters with an almost extra-terrestrial aspect, characterized by their large heads and small body frames. These beguiling characters also have some distant parentage in the paintings of Paula Rego. Usually starting out from photographs of friends, Tuesday translates these into a few sketches and then transfers her final image onto canvas where she begins painting with acrylics. The finely executed detailing of the face is achieved by subtle use of tone and shade, and the realism of the delineation only adds to the novelty and attraction of her characters. The focus on their wide-spaced eyes which are almost at the side of their head, has affinities with fondly remembered childhood marionettes. As presented here, her figures seem to have all the styled self-consciousness of children dressing up and fashionably aping their parents. The posturing of the bespectacled friends is calculatedly framed to capture our attention as we ponder their tortoise-like straining heads and stares. Similarly, the startling raven-haired girl overleaf takes on an almost bovine appearance as she stares out from the frame.

HARLEM BUNNY 2003

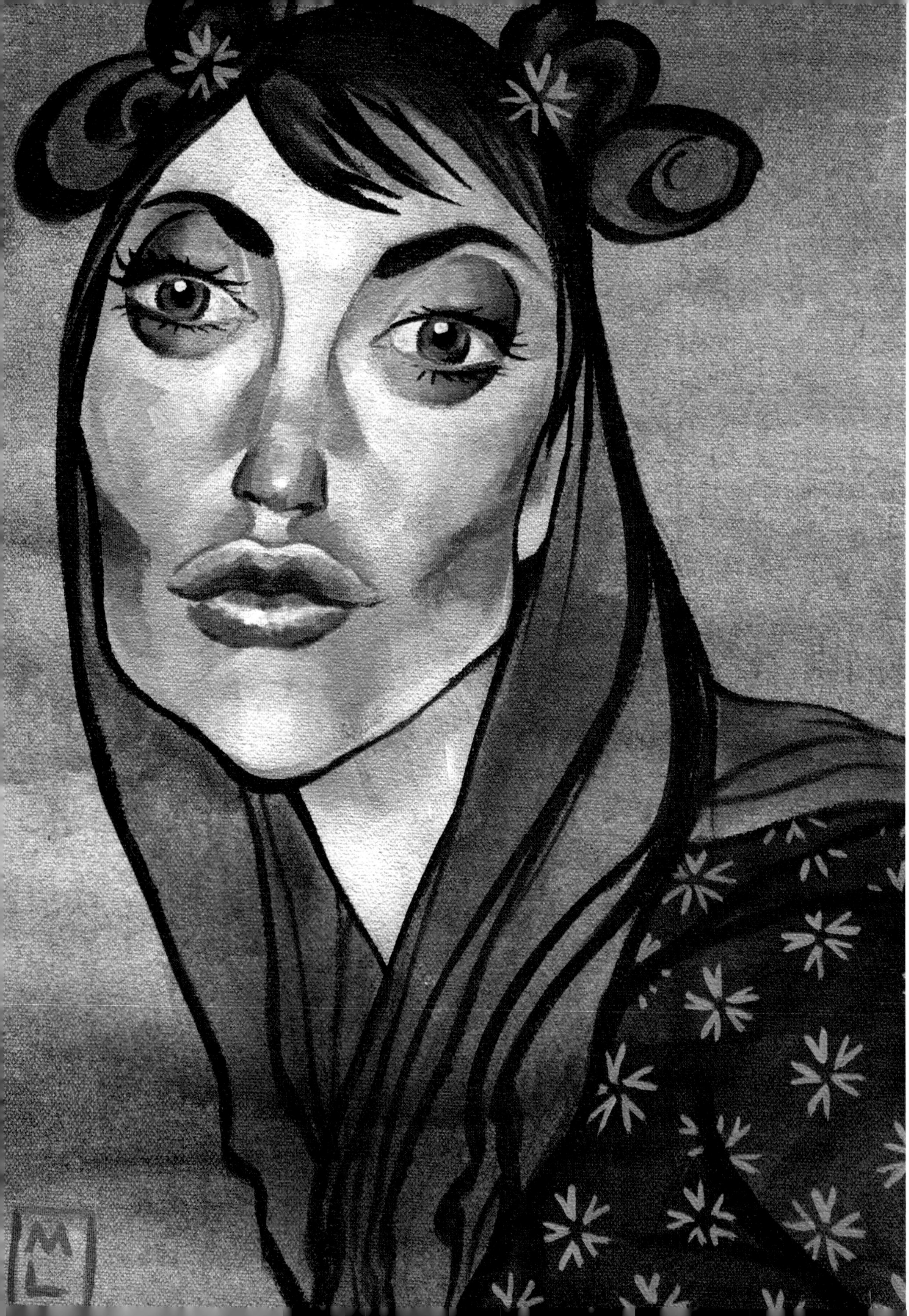

UNTITLED 2003

I see fashion becoming more and more about the individual and how a specific personality wants to uniquely portray him or herself not only through what they wear, but also how they choose to wear it. It is not so much about the person conforming to the clothes as it is fashion conforming to a personality or an underground counter culture. This is what I aim to achieve in my illustrations.

HERMAN YAP

SINGAPORE

LASALLE-SIA, SINGAPORE
UNIVERSITY OF NEW SOUTH WALES, SYDNEY, AUSTRALIA

Constantly elaborating on his vivid memories of people and places he has seen, Herman injects a large amount of the fantastical into his stylized illustration. His imagination is not restrained by the everyday, rather he creates flights of fancy that vividly project his personal belief that "design depicts individuality." Herman usually starts with raw sketches that are then scanned into the computer. His digital illustrations are a combination of photo-imaging and vector line using Adobe Photoshop and Macromedia Freehand. The images are lovingly rendered with a beautician's attention to make-up and facial detail. In particular the ever-sparkling eyes are singled out for special treatment. The decorative framing of the figures is reminiscent of the hand-painted photographic pieces of Pierre et Gilles, which carry a similar narrative element.

FLOWER POWER 2001

My illustrations are usually based on my imagination, memories, and fantasies. I draw inspiration from fashion photographers like Richard Avedon, David LaChapelle, and Pierre et Gilles, with reference to their art direction and innovative concepts. I liken my illustrations to photography as I have total control over how my models appear to the viewer.

COSMIC DOLL 2003

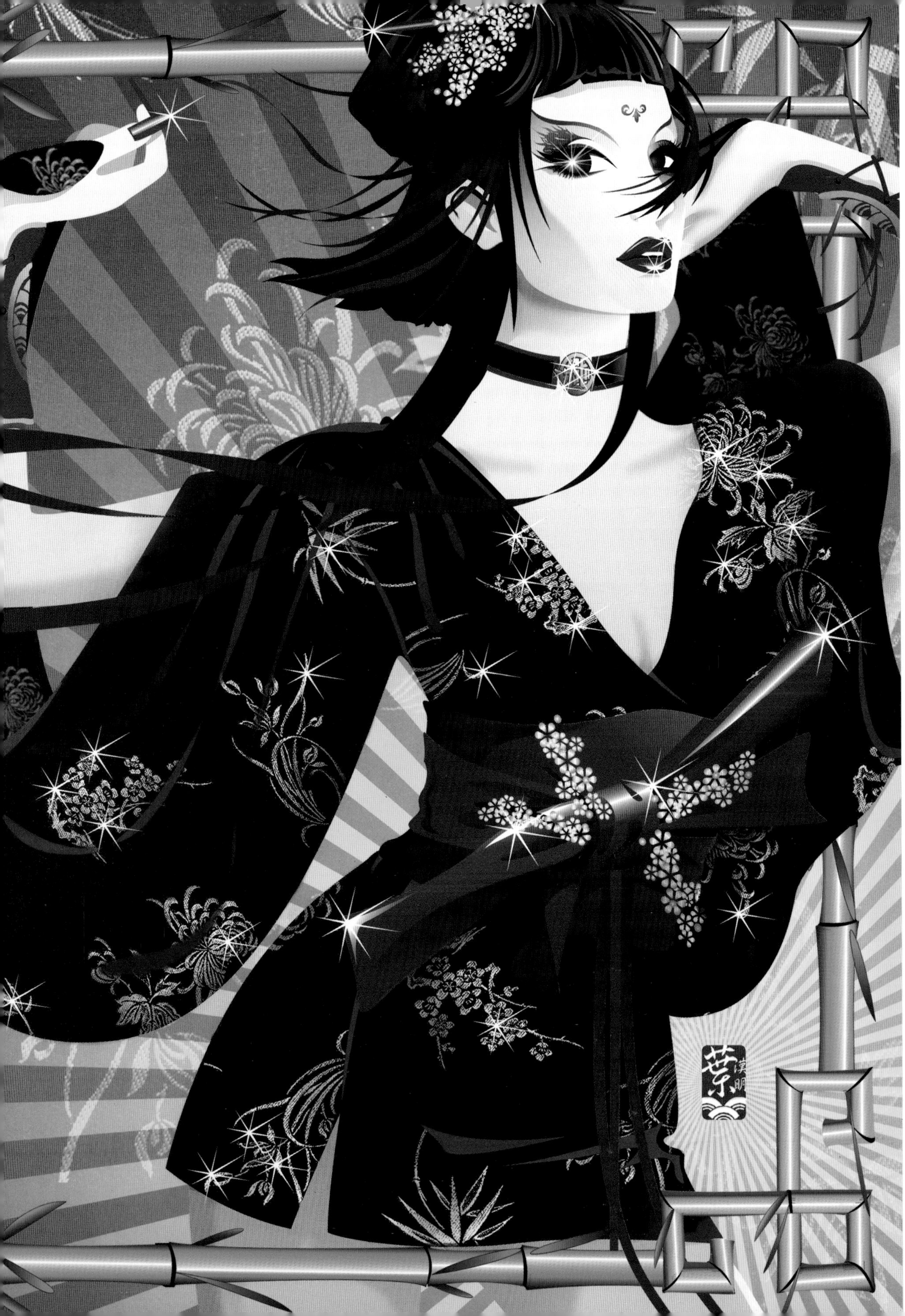

GEISHA 2003

CLAIBOURN HAMILTON

CONTEMPORARY WOMAN WITH SUNGLASSES 2003

USA
FASHION INSTITUTE OF TECHNOLOGY, NEW YORK, USA
ACADEMY OF ART COLLEGE, SAN FRANCISCO, USA

The rarefied aura of the glamorous celebrity is well captured in these fashion portraits. People fascinate Claibourn, and working with them every day continually inspires him to capture their various emotions, identities, and expressions. He starts with preliminary pencil sketches, then the computer takes over as he manipulates his image in Adobe Photoshop. In the tradition of Richard Bernstein's mega-star celebrity portraits, Claibourn's work responds to the current fascination of documenting the rich and famous. Usually employing photographs as a starting point, each figure is realistically etched with stylized, clean, descriptive lines to achieve dramatic results. The reliance on solid colour is complemented by the introduction of simple light and shade to lift the figure from its 2-D colouring-book appearance. The flowing locks of pop icon Beyoncé sweep across the page as someone in the crowd catches her eye. In contrast, the young male fan cloaks himself by shrouding his head with a hood.

CONTEMPORARY MALE IN HOOD 2003

I live in New York City... that alone heightens and stimulates my reaction to contemporary culture on a much higher scale. My exposure to people, fashion, culture, ethnicity, art, and sexuality comes in a very concentrated form in this city.

SHO MURASE

JAPAN

VANCOUVER FILM SCHOOL, CANADA

CENTRE D'ESTUDIS CINEMATOGRAFICS DE CATALUNYA
BARCELONA, SPAIN

ESCOLA SUPERIOR DE DISSENY I D'ART LA LLOTJA
BARCELONA, SPAIN

There is a recognizable mix of cross-cultural references in Sho's exquisitely structured and detailed illustrations. Although of Japanese and Korean origin, she grew up in Spain where, after studying psychology, she was seduced into pursuing graphic design in Barcelona and, later on, animation in Vancouver. It is simple to spot the influences of the decorative styles of Gustav Klimt and Alphonse Mucha that are overlapped with the work of graphic Japanese comic artist Yoshitaka Amano and the animé wizardry of Koji Morimoto. These striking images of stylish, highly individual dress begin as hand-drawings in pencil, then are scanned into the computer to be painted using Adobe Photoshop. The richness of the transformation is adroitly attained, leaving compositions that provide both dramatic visual impact and eye-catching elegance.

COVER *SEI* MAGAZINE 2003

DEATH & LEGEND

COVER *SEI* MAGAZINE 2003

SEI
Death & Legend

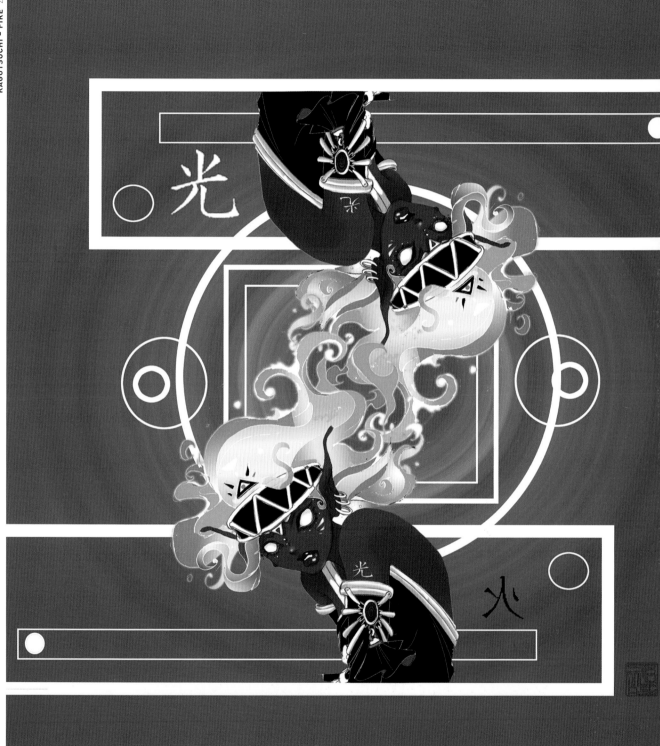

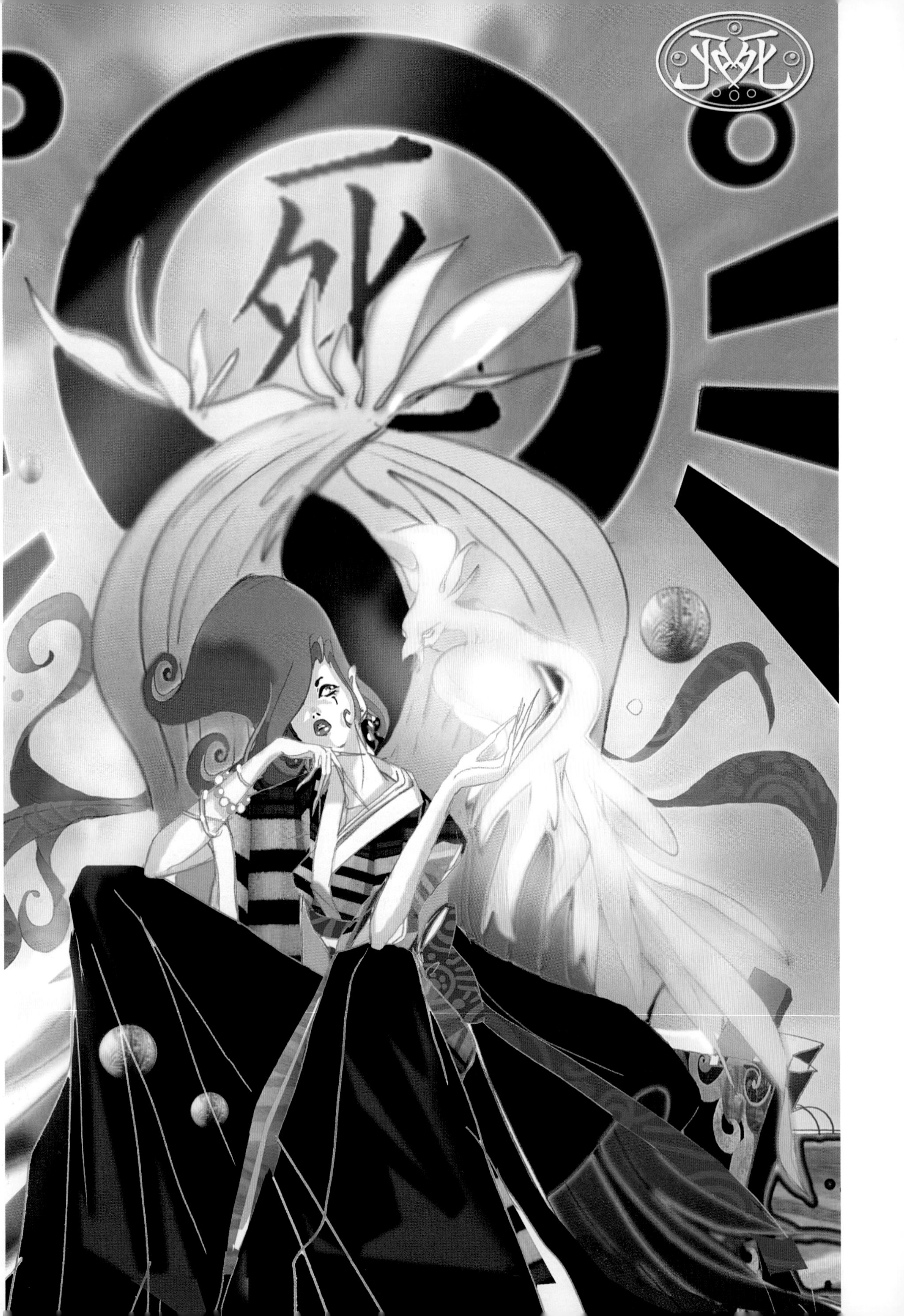
死

As with all art forms, fashion is slowly blending across the world... yet, each country still has its own style and needs, and so has every city. My work is heavily influenced by other art forms, especially animation and comics. It aims to reflect the blend of cultures I have been exposed to myself.

KAGUTSUCHI – FIRE MANDALA 2002

PEARL BATES

UK

CENTRAL ST MARTINS COLLEGE OF ART & DESIGN, LONDON, UK

BRIGHTON COLLEGE OF TECHNOLOGY, UK

Pearl's elegant ladies are beautifully realized from a rich recipe of acrylic, ink, oil, and pencil. Drawing inspiration from the people she sees around her in the street or at parties, Pearl's obvious delight in and exploration of colour is loaded with potent sensuality. In fact the mood she evokes seems more akin to an opulent natural world of exotic birds and luxuriant flowers rather than the world of fashion. The warming hues of the colour palette are well exploited in a generous mark-making technique that is almost Expressionist in style. The elongated canvases emphasize the slender figures which have the poised elegance of Art Nouveau figures. These stylish females are conscious of their allure and play upon the viewer as skilfully as cinematic vamps.

KAZUKO 2002

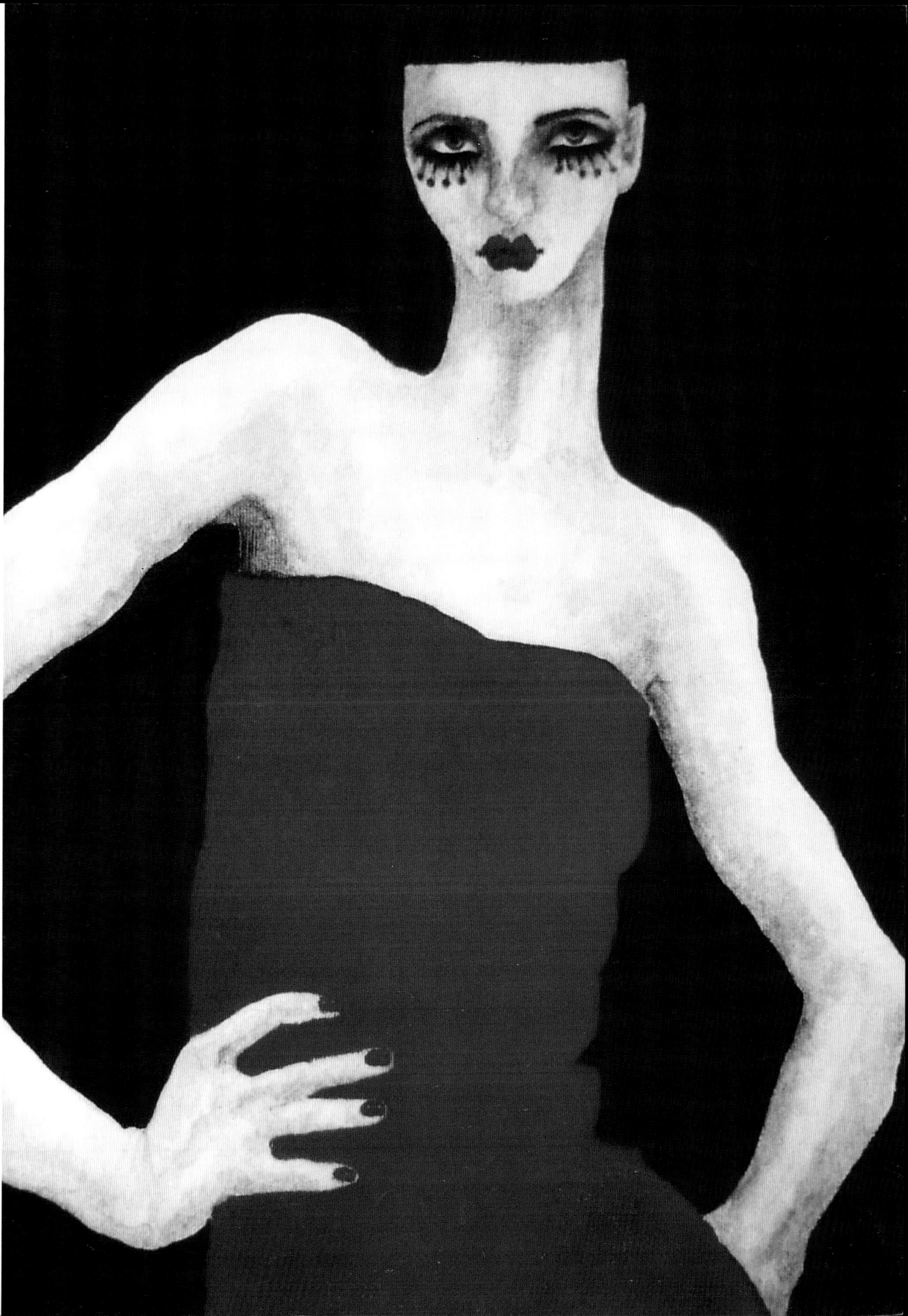

I believe we have an emotional need for fantasy, glamour, and beauty, and fashion is a way for us to express this need. It creates a whole dreamworld full of enchantment, desire, and intoxication into which we can escape. Expressing this world through paint touches the alchemy of our passion for fashion.

ALEK 2003

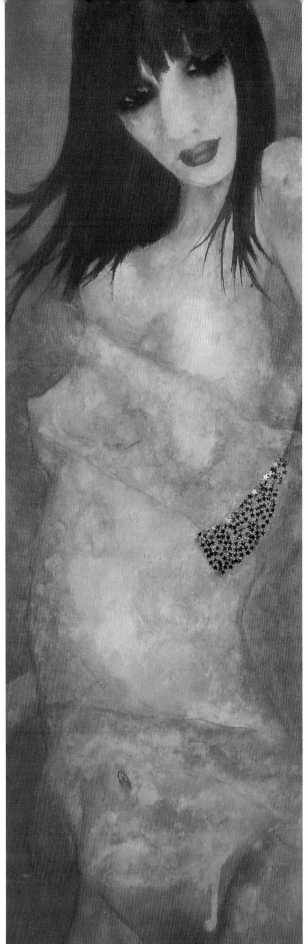

ROBERT WEISS

USA

RICHARD STOCKTON STATE COLLEGE OF NEW JERSEY, USA

Fashions come and go, but I think what really matters is the individual style a person develops. People are more fashion-conscious than ever, so it's fascinating to see how they put things together. That's something that definitely influences my work. Nothing is more inspirational to me than a smartly dressed woman.

Robert's graphically executed females look like contenders for the eye-candy role in the latest James Bond movie. Robert confesses to thumbing through lots of magazines to provide inspiration, and explains that music and movies have a big effect on his illustrations. Working exclusively on his Macintosh, everything is created on the computer, as Robert prefers not to scan in preliminary drawings. Occasionally he uses a drawing tablet to render work. He uses Adobe Illustrator to provide his very flat, clean, stylized look. There is more than a token glance toward the world of Mel Ramos in these images of scantily clad females which exude a style more often reserved as the territory of the glamour photographer. Robert is self taught, and his work is often reminiscent of the techniques and posturing of 1950s' pulp- fiction cover artists. His figures are usually framed against tonally related furniture and backgrounds, the use of colour remains restrained and diluted, adding a characteristic personal flavour.

ORB CHAIR 2003

AMY HOWARD

UK
NORTHUMBRIA UNIVERSITY, NEWCASTLE, UK

Amy's illustrations have tremendous vigour in both the use of applied media and her energetic drawing. There is also a suggestion of graffiti art in the liberal use of sprayed overlays and backgrounds. Amy has a refreshing, free approach to depicting the fashion image. The sketches are carried out with an energy that contrasts with the static pose of the subjects. This is not a cleanly etched, stereotypical representation of the female form. In a style with roots in the work of the Dadaists, the photo-realistic representation of the face is vandalized with the indiscriminate overprinting of colour and random scribbling with Biro. The eyes are emphasized with circles giving them a birdlike appearance. This work challenges the traditional face of accepted beauty.

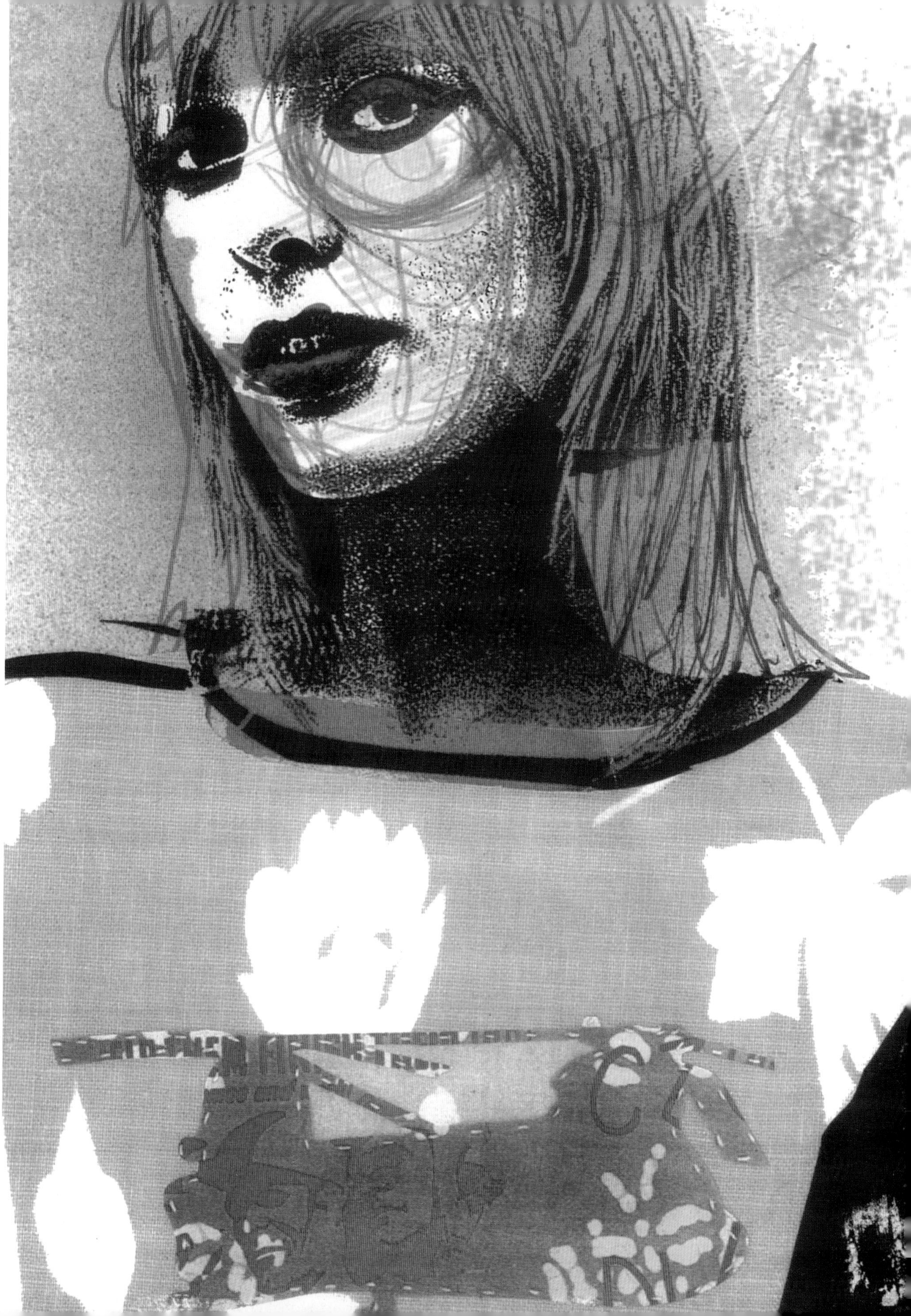

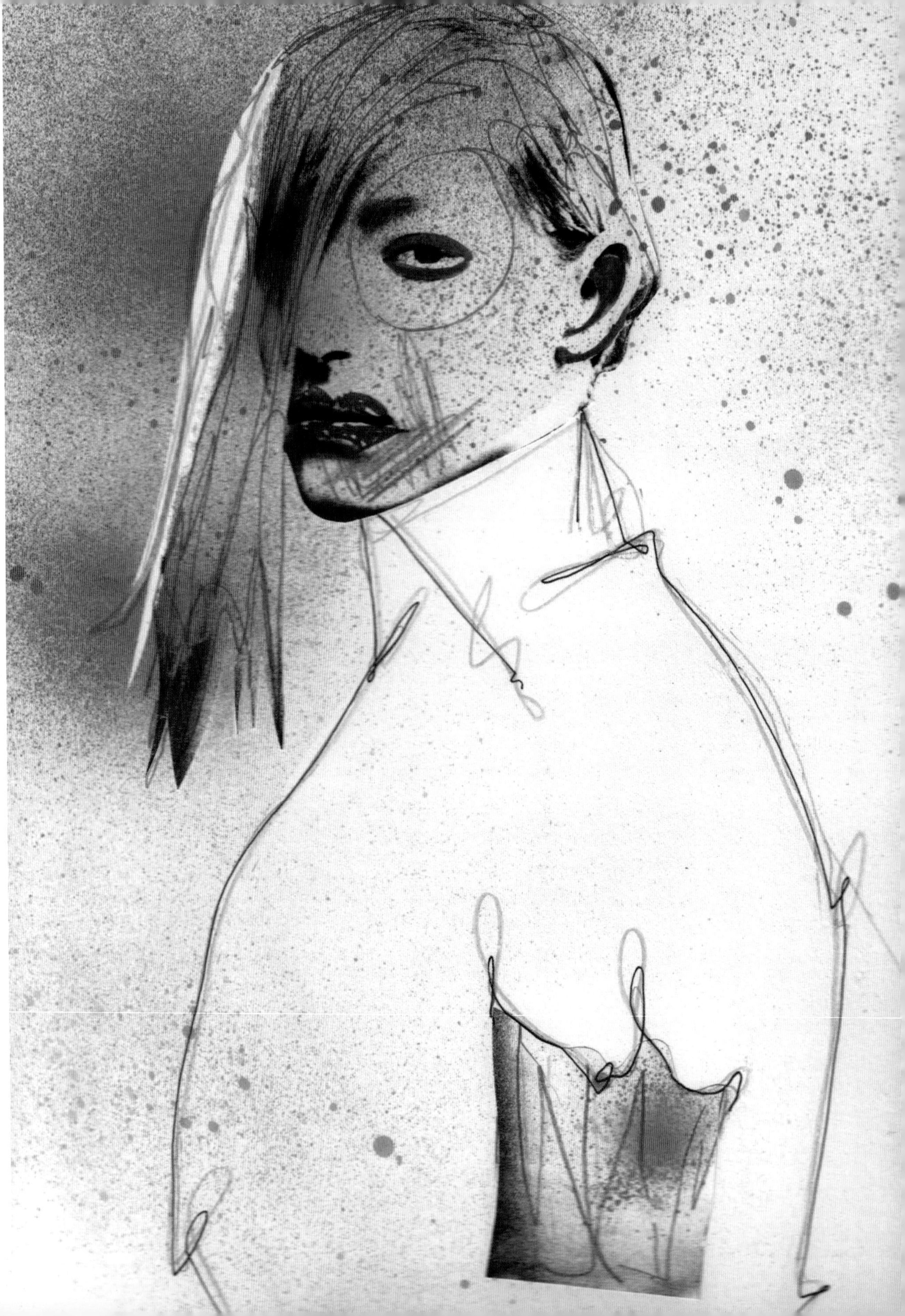

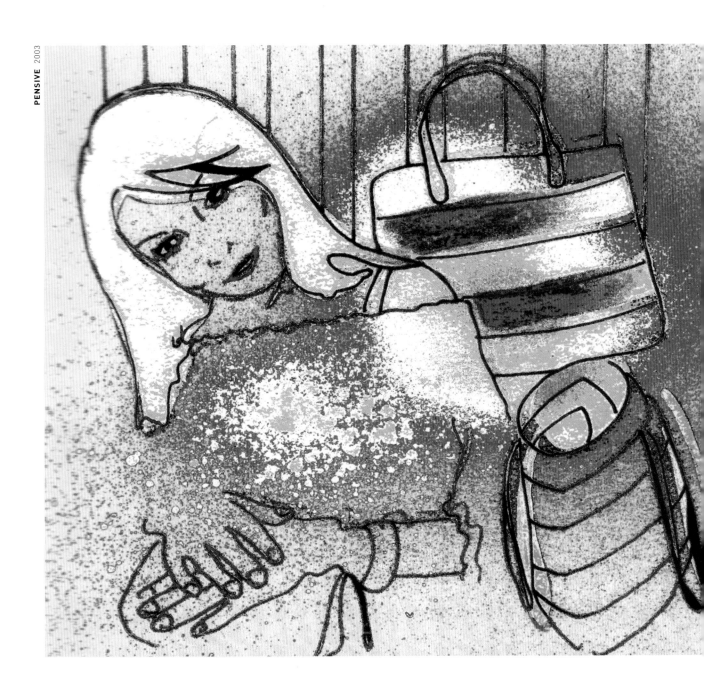

My illustrations are not to be taken too seriously, they are merely fun, thought-provoking images. The erratic Biro scribble makes the onlooker wonder why the image isn't perfect. We all aim for perfection, but the only person who can rate that perfection is ourselves, as another person's idea of perfection may not be our own. Being perfect is not the answer; striving to be ourselves is.

The radical changes brought about by digital communication have predictably had an impact on the promotional face of design. This places a question mark over the future communication of fashion's new identities. It has taken some persuasion for the fashion establishment to accept these advances but, as technology enriches the possibilities of experimentation, more have responded to, and eventually taken up, the challenge. It has become apparent that to stay ahead in the innovation stakes, fashion has to embrace new technological advances.

In 1997 Belgian designer Martin Margiela upturned the fashion apple cart by deconstructing second-hand clothes and reassembling them, only to spoil them again by applying bacteria. His gauntlet challenge, flaunted in the accepted face of fashion, has been maintained by current avant-garde designers and has resulted in a reappraisal of fashion that had previously spent too long looking over its shoulder at the past.

There had been rumblings of discontent when Issey Miyake's visionary 1983 exhibition, *Bodyworks*, saw him cast laminated polyester breastplates and sculpt body cages from rattan.

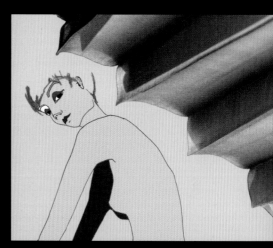

Miyake's investigations have now come full circle in his revolutionary A-POC (A Piece of Cloth) in which the customer creates their own garment from a roll of prepared fabric. This influence from the East paved the way for Yohji Yamamoto and Rei Kawakubo's Comme des Garçons to assault the traditional values of Western fashion.

Alexander McQueen has since constructed garments from metal; Donna Karan has made paper cocktail frocks; Hussein Chalayan has designed "aeroplane dresses" from fibre glass and resin. Digital implants into cloth manufacture are destined to allow future designers to provide wearable computing.

The promotion and styling of these clothes demands an exploration of new avenues of presentation. Challenging catwalk preconceptions, Jean-Paul Gaultier started using ordinary people instead of the stereotypical runway supermodel; Martin Margiela took his clients out to shows in the waste ground of the Paris suburbs; while John Galliano commandeered the Gare d'Austerlitz for the delivery of his models by steam train.

Everything seemed to force an equivalent style of 2-D presentation. Digital photography allowed

a degree of manipulation of the captured image that had previously been denied. Presentation of fashion – whether in the shop window, glossy magazine, or on billboards – rose to this challenge with increasing invention. Photographers like Guy Bourdin and David LaChapelle established a new flavour of fashion styling, while, in the sphere of advertising, Benetton's Oliviero Toscani outraged the world with his shocking billboard images.

The same experimentation is evident on the internet. Nick Knight's pioneering website www.showstudio.com describes itself as a fashion multimedia workshop, and relishes the chance to apply shock tactics in relaying the immediacy of fashion. The multimedia trend predictions of Lidewij Edelkoort fully embrace technology and are as demanding as any fine art installation. The trade prediction publications and journals *Viewpoint*, *View on Colour*, and *Bloom*, and style information resources WGSN and Promostyl have all embraced new media to document fashion and textile design in new and exciting ways.

The illustrators featured in this section are similarly out to challenge convention in their representation of fashion in all its mannerisms.

BORJA URIONA URIARTE

SPAIN
UNIVERSITY OF THE BASQUE COUNTRY, LEJONA, SPAIN
LONDON COLLEGE OF PRINTING, UK
UNIVERSITY OF EAST LONDON, UK

In line with the current revival of handmade objects, Borja's fabric collages convincingly describe the male peacock's weekend wardrobe. The casual dress code is fluently complemented by the technique of cut and sew, using pronounced appliqués of texture and fabric. The visual culture of R B Kitaj and Richard Hamilton's photographic imagery are acknowledged influences on Borja's style. These characteristically bold fabric paintings are developed in the main from cloth scraps sourced in local markets and charity shops. Borja started by drawing images in flat colours using gouache and acrylics, and then began to experiment with different fabrics. The figures are skilfully sculpted together with the use of differing materials to denote form and shade. The uninterrupted regularity of the horizontal pinstripe backgrounds contrasts well with the free expression of the clothes and figures.

I have always been interested in American Western culture – cowboys, horses, the landscape of the Grand Canyon.

NATURAL CHIC 2003

FIONA WYLIE

UK

LEEDS METROPOLITAN UNIVERSITY, UK

These figures are articulated with a seductive posturing reminiscent of the provocative linear fashion illustrations of Julie Verhoeven. Fiona currently takes her subject inspiration from magazines, although she intends to enrich her reference by incorporating her own styled photography. Each composition is developed by hand, working first in pencil and then in Rotring pen. The resulting silhouette is either left empty or flooded with solid colour, and the computer is used to emphasize its clean and elegant outline. Fiona's expressive technique is free and delicate using a descriptive line that travels fluently across the page, etching out her subject in the sophisticated manner of a romanticized Aubrey Beardsley drawing. There is a pungent undercurrent of stimulating, sensual emotion within each illustration. Fiona's figures are frequently caught off-camera, in unguarded moments, lost within their personal flights of fancy. These day-dreaming, often psychedelic, characters lure us into shaking off the mundane to escape with them into their own furtive worlds.

Through my illustrations, I am continually in pursuit of capturing the informal beauty of our existence. I attempt to present the mundane on an elevated and sublime level, portraying the most ordinary of objects in a mysterious and intriguing manner. My work has a romantic, often erotic, current that runs through each linear description. I aspire to give the familiar the impressiveness of the unfamiliar.

TUESDAY AFTERNOON AT LUCY'S 2003

ANTON STOREY

UK

DOMUS ACADEMY, MILAN, ITALY
LIVERPOOL JOHN MOORES UNIVERSITY, UK

Anton's beautifully drawn figures express a half-revealed, dreamlike existence. His fluid line etches his females with the simplest suggestion of restrained form and outline. This evocative and sensitive approach is complemented by subtle lines and gradations of shade. The sensitive line is vaguely reminiscent of the sinewy crayoning of Egon Schiele or the sensual portraiture of Mel Odom. The faces are stylized with mask-like severity, sometimes with only one eye, and are fleshed out with single shades and tones. They give the impression of unfinished sketches, yet each seems complete. The compositions are carefully balanced as weight and information are reduced to allow the drawing to absorb into the page.

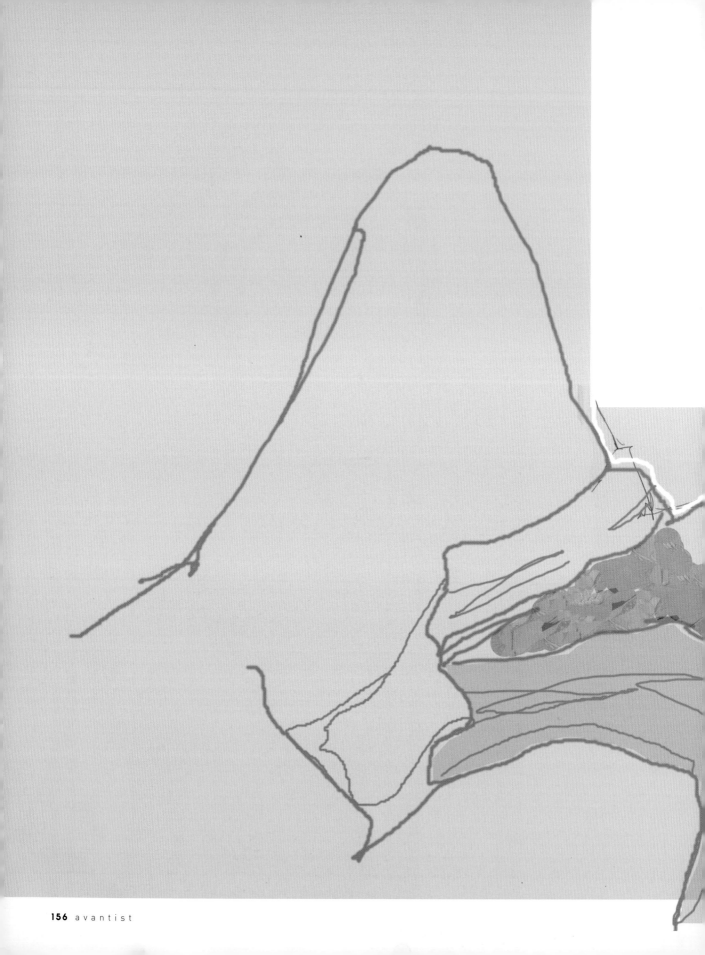

In my illustration work, I try to instil realism into what is essentially a fantasy – basically the reverse of what a photographer does. I aim to capture and confine feeling and inject something intangible into the constraints and composition of a photograph, or 2-D statement. While the photographer interprets and transforms what is fundamentally a model and garment, I try to reinvent what is unattainable in reality to achieve something more believable.

MiKi AMANO

JAPAN

PARSONS SCHOOL OF DESIGN, NEW YORK, USA

I am attracted to things I find cute and contrary: the fluffy fur on a scrawny cat, the colourful feathers on a squawking bird, and the intricate patterns on a poisonous snake. Humans use fashion for decoration and to express their idiosyncracies.

Miki's background in textile design and the emphasis on colour in her work has given rise to her creating fun and original fashion illustration. She is passionate about drawing and is constantly doodling in her sketchbooks. She uses anything from crayons, paint, and silk-screen cut-outs, to multimedia and digital software to realize her illustrations. She likes to collect photographs from retro magazines to source her moody narrative images. Her assemblies spark their own special identity. The upturned coffee cup as a dress, characteristic of the surreal technique of Salvador Dalí and René Magritte, seems a perfect hallucinatory garment solution for this 1950s' housewife. The collaged kitchen scene inventively mixes together both sketched and photographic images within a staged perspective of simple blocked colour and repeated pattern.

COFFEE LADY 2002

SARAH BEETSON

UK
FALMOUTH COLLEGE OF ARTS, UK

Sarah's images, with their bustling energy and innovation, are a reflection of herself. Obsessed by fashion and inspired by everything from vintage clothing to 1980s' Pepsi logos, these subjects now infuse her life to the point where she openly admits to dressing like her illustrations. Sarah is particularly fascinated by man-made, commercial sites that have lost their shiny new surface and have fallen into disrepair. She has a lifelong obsession with the seedy intimacy of fairgrounds (her favourites being Coney Island in Brooklyn, New York, and Brighton, UK). There is an aftertaste of this in these cluttered portraits of bubblegum divas and drag queens. Typographical ideas are also often incorporated. Working primarily in mixed media Sarah generates proof trials on paper, often using her own styled photo-shoots of friends as her starting point. The results are usually rendered onto wood, incorporating gouache, acrylic, and spray-paint. These are further embellished with applied elements including tissue paper, sequins, buttons, candy, and sweet wrappers. The palette is flamboyant in its exploration of colour, and the use of confectionary pinks and reds adds exoticism into the mix. Jean-Michel Basquiat's similarly fragmented and chaotic paintings are a clear influence.

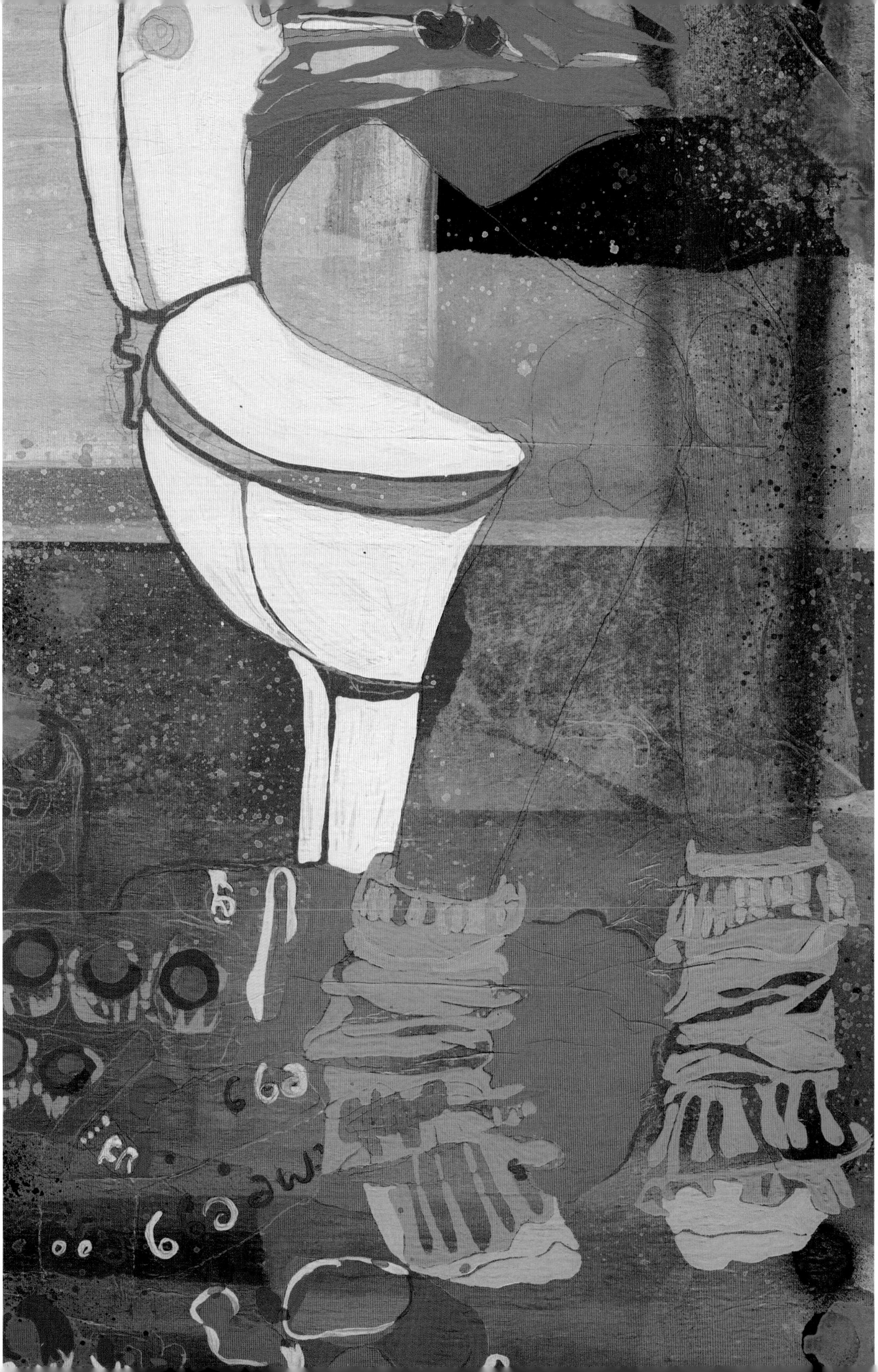

TOILET FEAST 2002

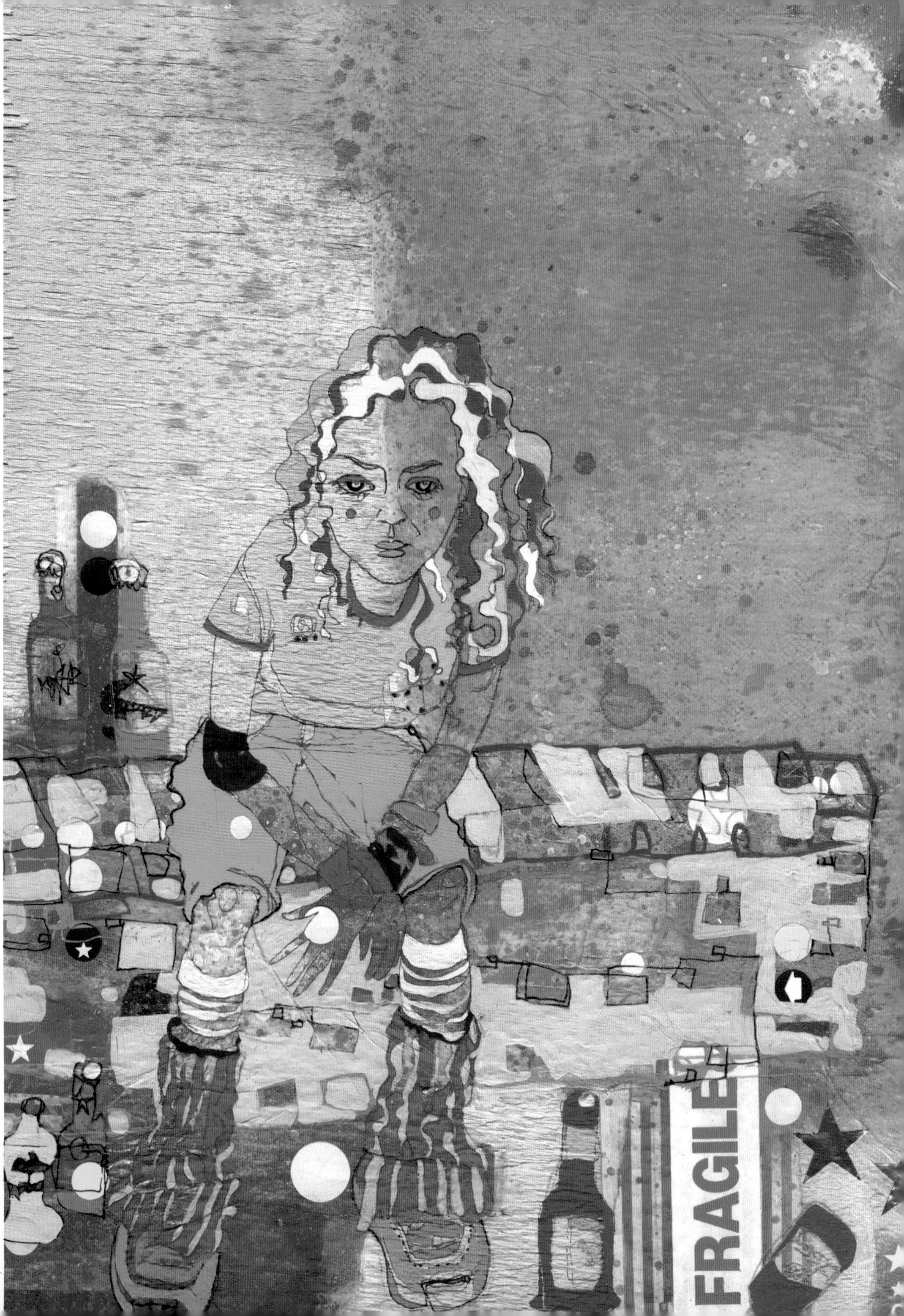
FRAGILE

I am interested in looking into the subcultures that derive from fashion, and I am particularly concerned with the portrayal of the darker elements that lie beneath its suface. Anorexia and bulimia nervosa, and playing with gender via make-up are persistent themes within my paintings; camouflaged beneath layers of sugar-sweet bubblegum colours and collaged elements.

WENDY MOODY

UK
MANCHESTER METROPOLITAN UNIVERSITY, UK
LIVERPOOL JOHN MOORES UNIVERSITY, UK

Working with a fertile imagination, Wendy conjures up fascinating and mysterious characters that unsettle the senses. These illustrations both attract and repel. They distort accepted values and also morph the ordinary into a surreal realization of contemporary dress. Inspired by childhood memories, old paintings, and movies, Wendy takes these ingredients and establishes her own personal perspective on fashion and style. She works from a variety of sketched and scanned objects, which she later assembles in layers in Adobe Photoshop. At first glance her images register as darkly complex but the nostalgia of a familiar children's doll appeals to the personal remembrances of the viewer. By providing these "models" with individual personality traits in their respective pose, dress, and hairstyles, Wendy steps outside the parameters of accepted style with a disturbing irreverence.

As a child I would close my eyes and imagine wearing the outfits I had seen in magazines and shops as a distraction from reality. Today we do not need to close our eyes, but just allow our dreams to become part of who and where we want to be.

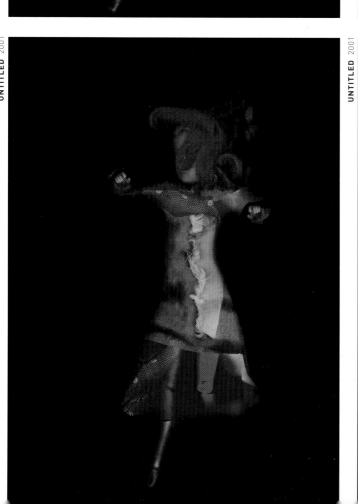

ANNA CANGIALOSI

USA

COLLEGE FOR CREATIVE STUDIES, DETROIT, USA
FASHION INSTITUTE OF DESIGN AND MERCHANDISING
LOS ANGELES, USA

Anna prepares her base by collaging the surface in tissues that provide subtle textures. There is a duskily veiled quality to these illustrations, which also have a recycled appeal. She usually uses gouache and acrylic in combination with papers and fabrics, photocopy transfers, and white-out. Working from a combination of her own imagination and sourced photographs, she is intrigued by the employment of line and the subtleties that can be achieved on a textured surface. Anna's sensual illustrations convey a delicate, transparent fragility, reminiscent of the sensitive drawings of Gustav Klimt with their sinewy, figurative aesthetic. The colour palette is muted, which adds to the contained atmosphere within each illustration. There are no strong contrasts, and the colours harmoniously blend and merge across the page. The vulnerability of the subject, partially dressed or in underwear, is sympathetically rendered with an understated expression.

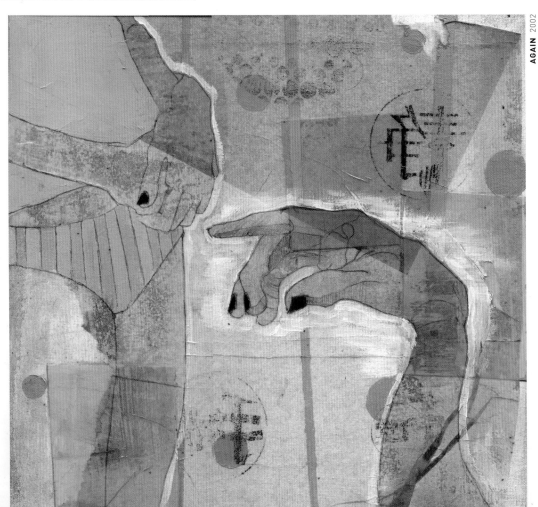

AGAIN 2002

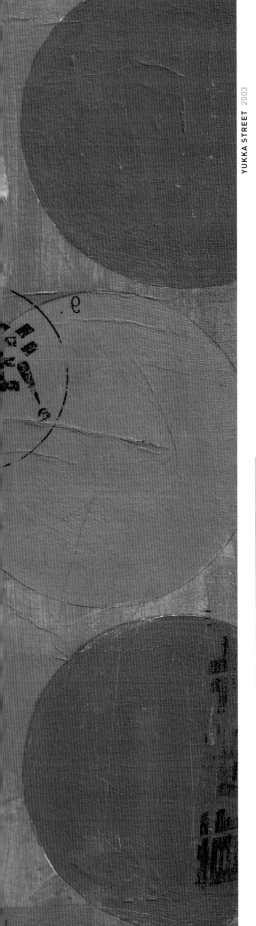

I choose to observe fashion in everyday environments. These settings depict figures, usually women, in combination with textures and pattern. The positioning of the figures is usually in stylized, awkward poses, not in traditional fashion poses. I find that clothing can be flattering in different ways when viewed at non-traditional angles.

SUSAN HIPPE

SOUTH AFRICA

ECOLE SUPERIEURE D'ARTS APPLIQUES DE TROYES, FRANCE

ECOLE D'ART DU HAVRE, FRANCE

ROEHAMPTON INSTITUTE, UK

Through a combination of progressive drawing, collage, and mixed media, Susan establishes a no-holds-barred impact with her forceful depictions of women. The rhythm of her draughtsmanship is choreographic in a technique that dizzyingly dances across the page with generous, sweeping gestures. A great hoarder of images, Susan confesses to stockpiling cupboards full of source material. Her drawings rarely remain as true replicas of these originals – indeed, often something quite different emerges. Her pen hits the surface running and leaves it in the same fashion. The spontaneous strength of line and colour vividly depict these proudly exhibitionist females. Her call girls, totally lacking any physical inhibitions, flaunt their sexuality as openly as Toulouse-Lautrec's risqué dance-hall soubrettes back in the 1890s. This one totters across the page balancing coyly on her elevating stilettos, while the horror of losing your underwear is convincingly caricatured in a sketch overleaf where the figure's facial expression is redolent of the satirical cartoons of the German Expressionist painter, George Grosz.

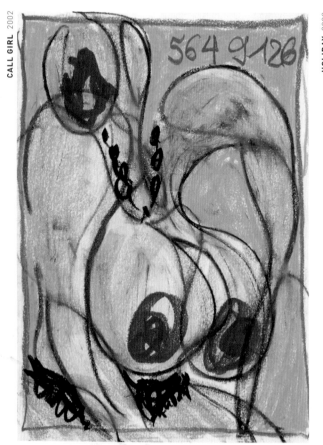

CALL GIRL 2002

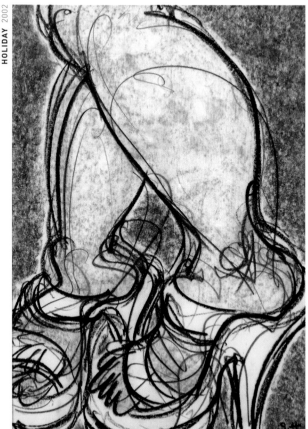

HOLIDAY 2002

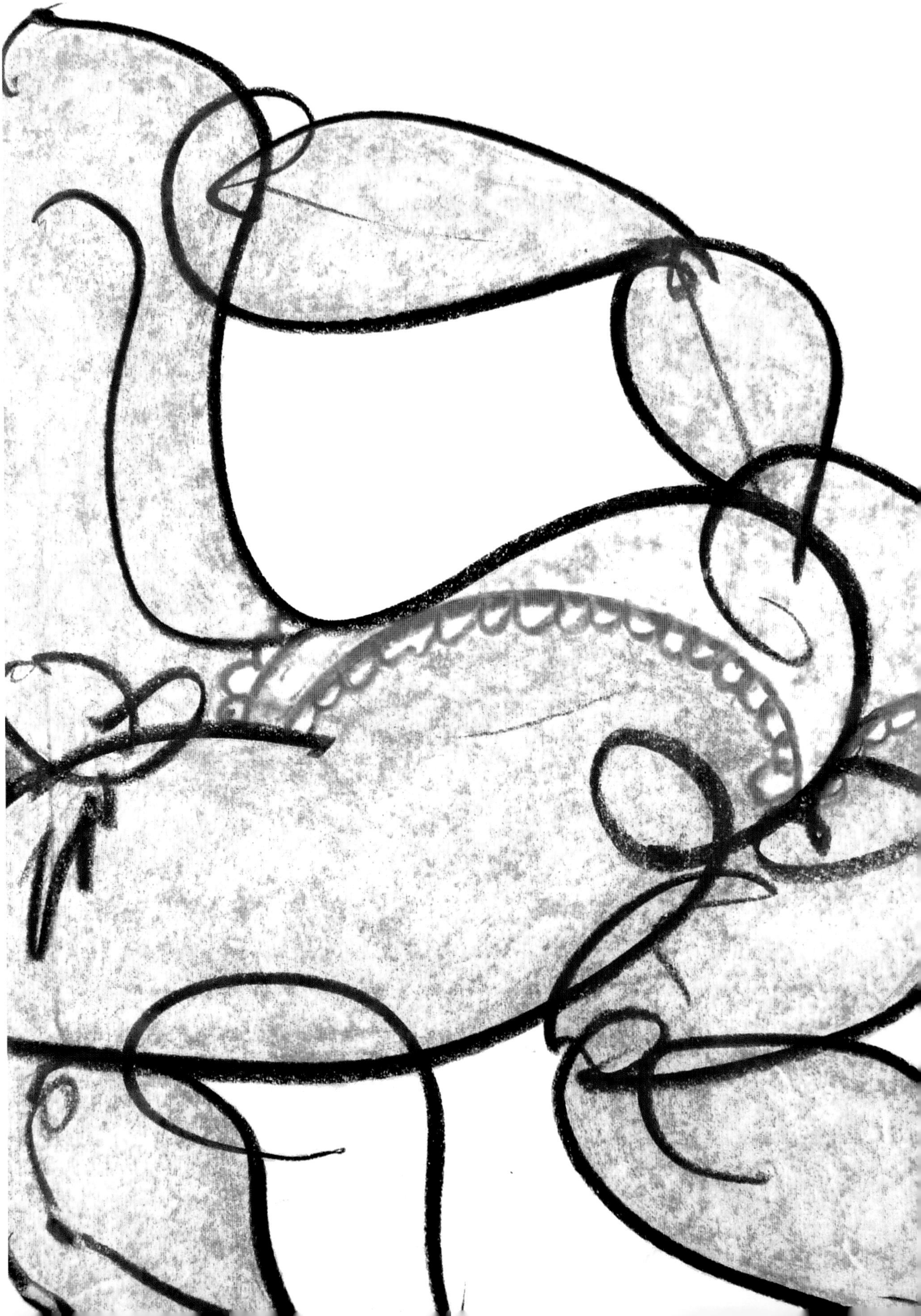

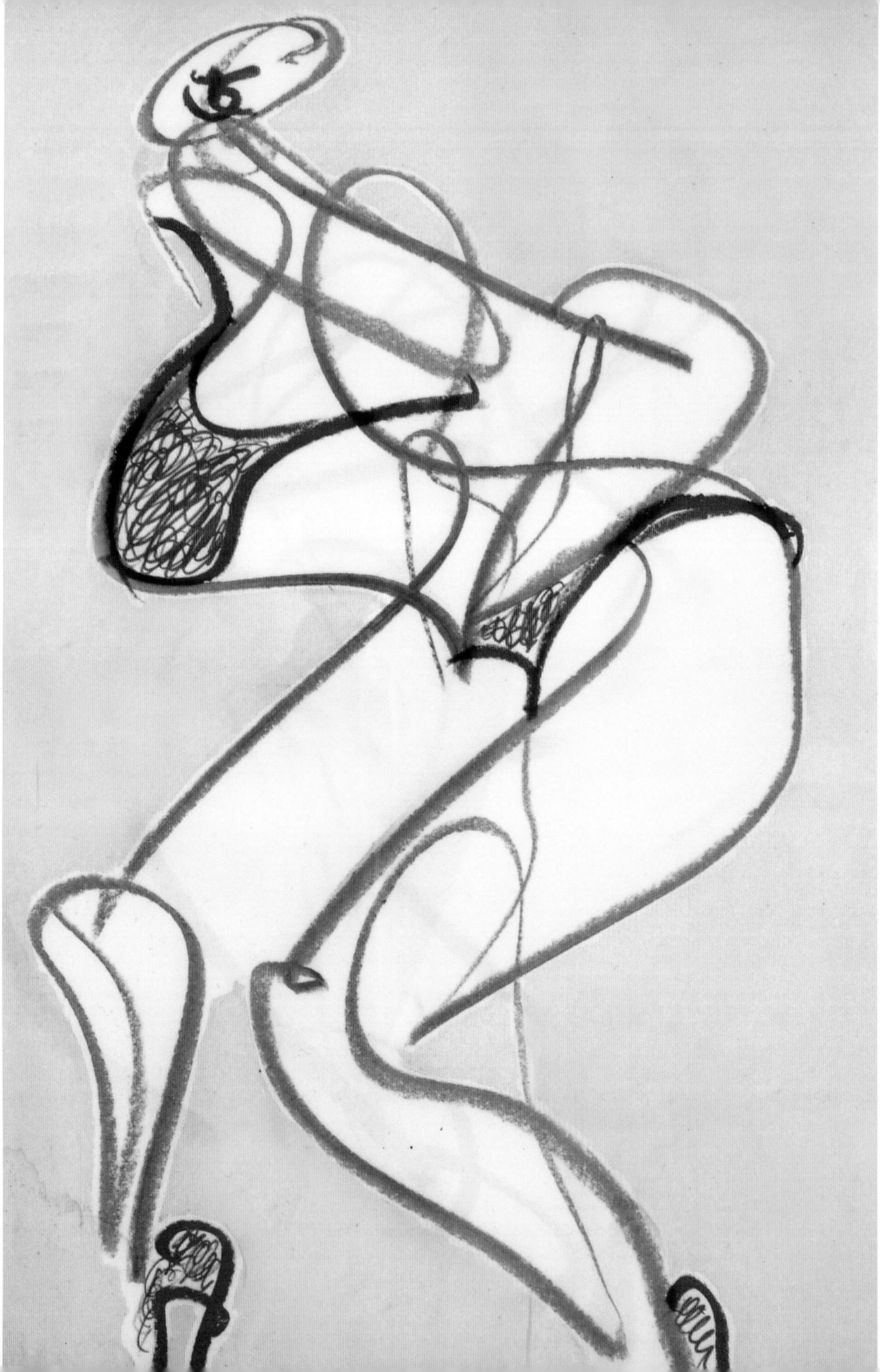

My drawings have no message other than to portray the funkiness of the world and my own intensity. My images are fast moving, energetic, positively mad, yet deep and powerful.

LOST MY KNICKERS 2001

VELVET UNDERGROUND 2002

ALISON ATKINS

UK
LIVERPOOL JOHN MOORES UNIVERSITY, UK

Alison's riotous, robotic couture mix is reminiscent of Oskar Schlemmer's geometric ballet figurines from the 1920s. Her simple, inert community is imaginatively conjured by photographically exposing *objets trouvés* that have been ingeniously pre-arranged to create a series of negative, abstracted store-window mannequins. The inspiration for this method was sparked by getting slightly bored working in the darkroom and experimenting with developing photographic negatives. The spontaneity of the technique is evident in the resulting ingenious images. The shrewd use of such easily recognizable trinkets enhances each figure with suggestions of each one's identity and persona. Their clothes are skilfully evoked by the subtle interplay of both transparent and solid textures within the clean articulation of each silhouette. Stacked like x-ray Barbie dolls, they are both trapped and frozen, waiting for the processing that will eventually allow them to step out of the box.

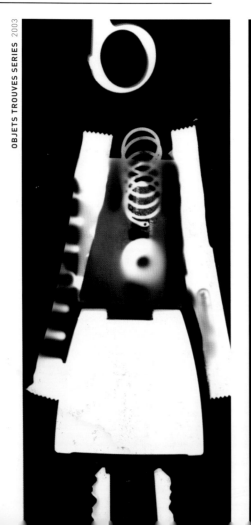
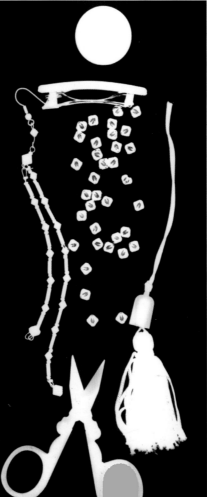
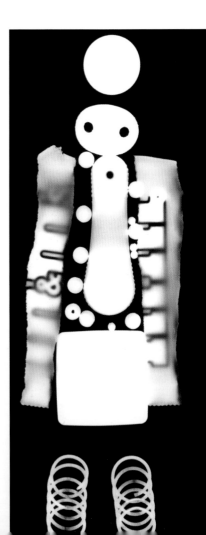

My individual observation of fashion design revolves around its exciting, diverse involvement with fabrics and styles. Yet the nature of fashion illustration is seen to be much less varied. I hope that the future holds a greater appreciation of individuality within illustration. I have learned to explore different drawing techniques and so my illustration is about disparity in the face of classical design disciplines – disproportional figures, bold and stylized stances, and no particular orientation of the garments.

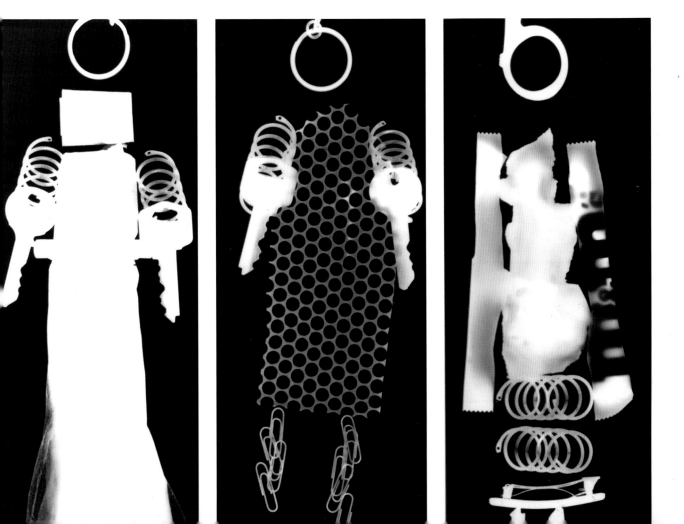

RICHARD MAY

UK · MANCHESTER METROPOLITAN UNIVERSITY

Although eventually employing digital software (Adobe Photoshop), Richard rarely draws directly on the computer, preferring to create preliminary drawings and textures away from the monitor screen. He relies on his trusty 'scraps box' to provide inspiration (found objects, corners of paintings, etc) in terms of visual reference and sometimes will resort to recycling his earlier illustrations. There is more than a trace of Allen Jones' visceral representation of women in these forceful illustrations. Similarly sexually provocative, Richard's own representation of the female form is offered with a reluctance to identify the face. The body-shaping garments and contours are the only clues to the gender of his subject. In the overlay of colour and texture these images also seem to draw upon Abstract Expressionism in their impulsive brushwork and spillage of colour.

LONDON YOGA GUIDE 2003

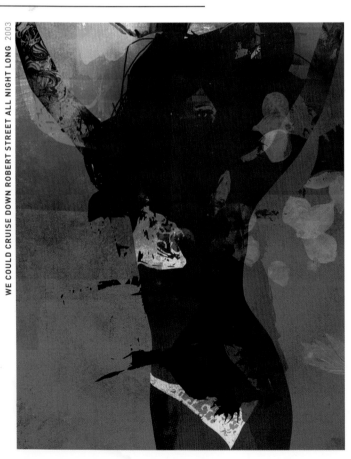

WE COULD CRUISE DOWN ROBERT STREET ALL NIGHT LONG 2003

Some days I'd rather chew gravel and sandpaper my testicles than watch MTV or flick through – purely for example – *The Face* magazine. But I'd happily take their money, so 15 minutes of each, once a month, usually does the trick.

It's a sensual, bold, and bare response to fashion. It's about the pose becoming the product or language.

Although Lidia currently employs a mixture of drawing, photography, and computer graphics when generating her illustrations, she plans to rely less on CAD in future work. Photo-realism sketches are cleverly integrated in these clever compositions that evoke the glamour of the couture image. The scrunched medley of rouched fabric, or the run of pleated cloth that is translated into a staircase, charm the senses with their refinement. These illustrations operate like visual puns, with more than a passing nod to the Dadaists who projected their own absurd sense of humour by collaging everyday objects into their pictures. There is a sophisticated wit at work in Lidia's illustrations, notably in the unusual combining of everyday materials with couture.

SQUEEZEBALL 2002

BALLGOWN 2002

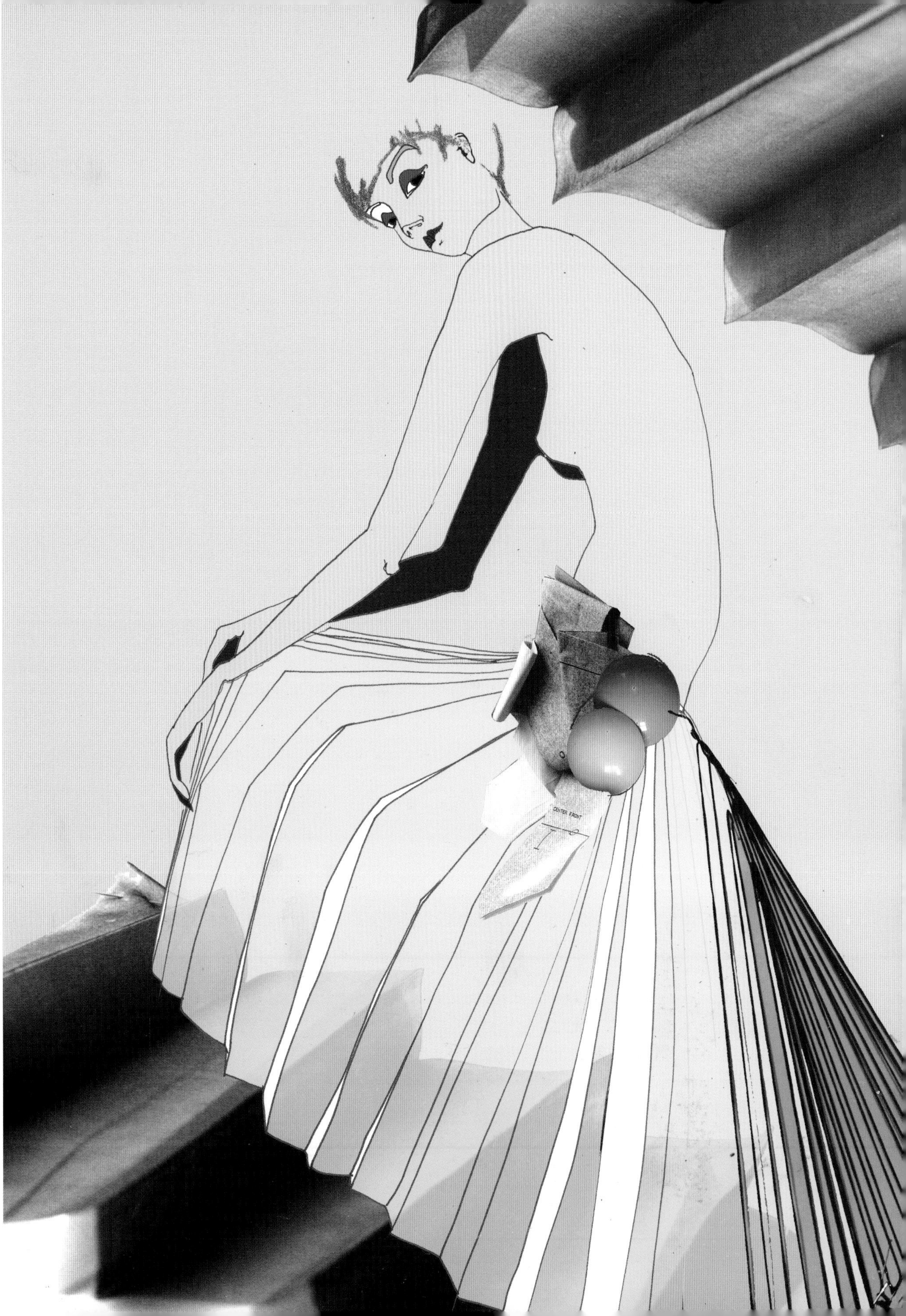
CENTER FRONT

LUCY MACLEOD

UK
EDINBURGH COLLEGE OF ART, SCOTLAND

Lucy makes a point of never throwing any magazines away. She hoards boxes of cut-out pictures and text from all types of publications for future inspiration. Many figures or faces come from pornographic magazines, as Lucy finds that these images convey much more real expression and have a specific narrative that she can play around with. She enjoys taking a photograph or sketch of a figure and reworking it so that it takes on a new meaning. She achieves this by focusing in on that person's identity – their emotions, motives, and desires. Aesthetically, there is a mixture of the traditional and the contemporary in these hand-drawn, painted, and digitally manipulated images. Lucy seems to relish the rough next to the smooth in her work which is perfumed with more than a whiff of Abstract Expressionism jumbled with a pungent measure of Pop Art. Lucy's illustrations assault our senses with their dramatic flair and assurance, teasing the viewer by taking the identifiable and framing it in a powerful new dynamic. These flamboyant pieces offer a unique reinterpretation of the accepted fashion image. Consumerism is evident overleaf in the repeated brand names of the New York shopper and in the endless racks of underwear. The images project their style as powerfully as billboard advertisements.

POSH BOY 2003

1st

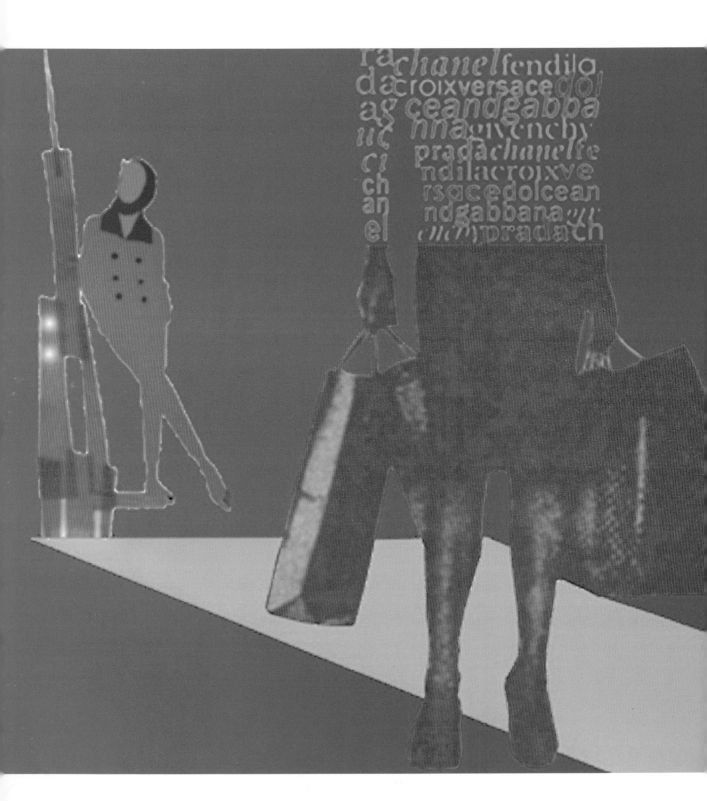

I see fashion as a never-ending game of pass-the-parcel... When the music stops, a designer peels off a layer, puts their stamp on it, and then passes it on for others to explore. It is a question of not being precious about what is high or low art and feeling free to alter an image's context or narrative to make it your own – all this while embracing the unfamiliar; that's what pushes boundaries forward.

EVA TATCHEVA

BULGARIA

ROYAL COLLEGE OF ART, LONDON, UK
KINGSTON UNIVERSITY, SURREY, UK

Eva delights the eye with a carnival of provocative images fused together with implication and hidden meaning. Her surreal representations distil a pulsating cocktail of realism together with phantasmagoric imagery and symbolic reference. Fruit is unashamedly exploited as a sexual metaphor. Manipulating a carefully restrained colour palette, Eva cultivates visual richness through the juxtaposition and assembly of her images. These lyrical arrangements fascinate the viewer with the sundry patterns and shapes that each illustration is pieced from. With similarities to Marc Chagall's paintings, these images create sophisticated similes behind a façade of fabled, childlike naïvety.

EDEN 1 2004

Fashion is about experimentation, exploration, changes, identity, and sexuality. I guess that is what attracts me to it. And I suppose this is what attracts many young people to fashion. Experimentation, change, identity, and sexuality make the world go round and, in this context, fashion plays an important and influential role.

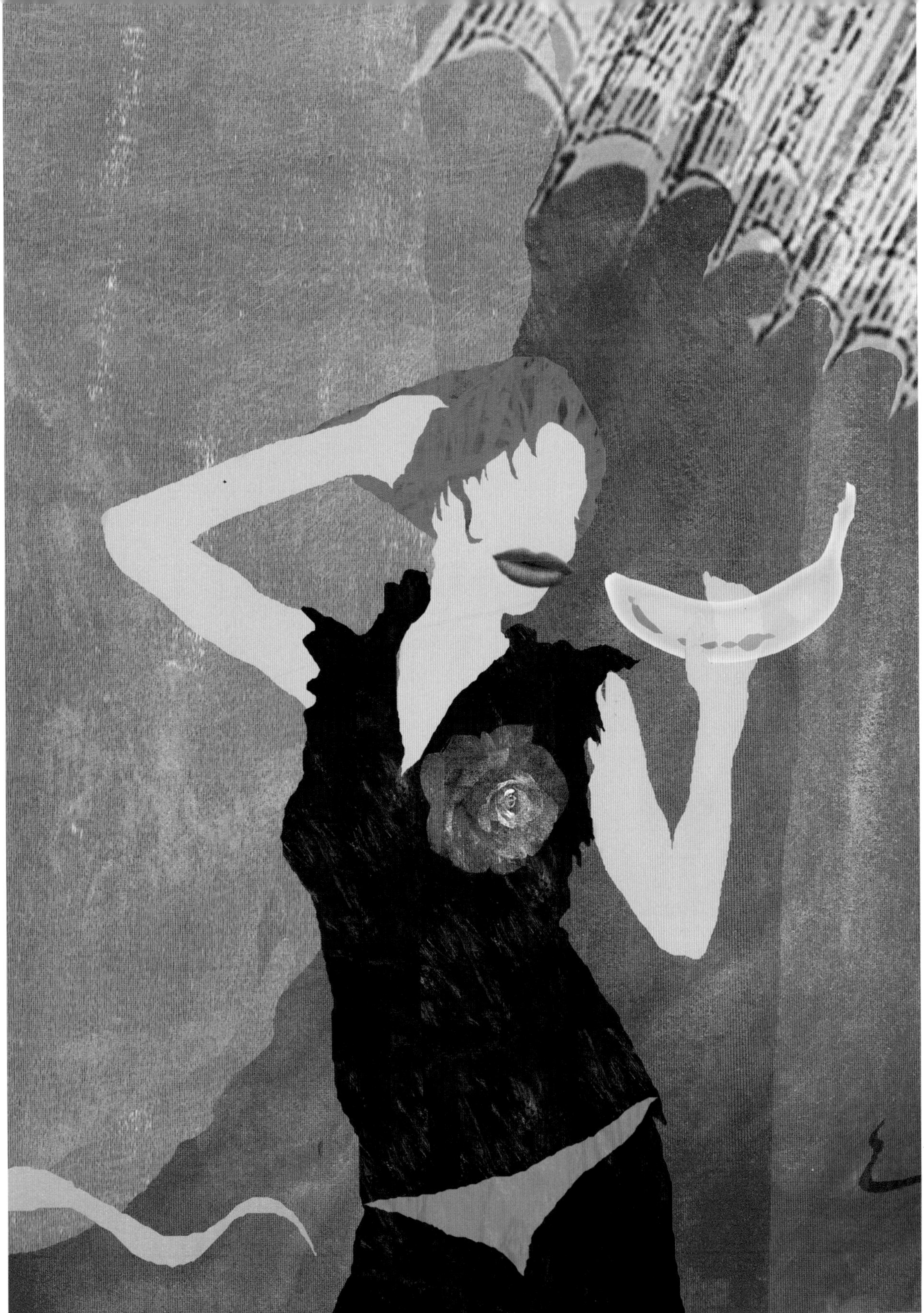

DANCE IN PINK 2004

Miki Amano
1-35-10-301 Tomigaya, Shibuya-ku
Tokyo, Japan,151-0063
Tel (Japan) +81 (3)3469 2122
Tel (US) +1 917 450 0056
mikiamano@mikiamano.com
www.mikiamano.com

Claire Anderson
38 Fullarton Crescent, Troon, Ayrshire
KA10 6LL, Scotland
Tel +44 (0)7753 282210
clairefrancesanderson@hotmail.com

Alison Atkins
79 Scalby Road, Scarborough
North Yorkshire, YO12 5QL, England
Tel + 44 (0)1723 377093
LSAAATKI@livjm.ac.uk

Pearl Bates
Redskap Cottage, Hamsey Lane
Cooksbridge, nr. Lewes, East Sussex
BN8 4SJ, England
Tel +44 (0)7760 222459
info@pearlbates.com
www.pearlbates.com

Sarah Beetson
69 Hadrian Way, Sandiway, Northwich
Cheshire, CW8 2JT, England
Tel +44 (0)7968 119183 /
+44 (0)20 7720 5202
sarahbeets@hotmail.com
Represented by Illustration Ltd
www.illustrationweb.com/sarahbeetson

Anna Cangialosi
annacangialosi@hotmail.com
www.altpick.com/annacangialosi

Alanna Cavanagh
93a Winchester Street, Toronto, Canada
Tel +1 416 515 0628
girlonabike@sympatico.ca
Represented by i2iart
Tel +1 888 277 7200
www.i2iart.com

Lidia Cerutti
l@lidiacerutti.com
www.lidiacerutti.com

Daniel Chen
eyepoop@sympatico.ca
Represented by i2iart
Tel +1 888 277 7200
www.i2iart.com

Marcos Chin
Tel +1 416 569 1983
marcoschin@hotmail.com
www.marcoschin.com

Nathalie Dion
Tel +1 514 725 1362
madame.dion@sympatico.ca
Represented by Anna Goodson
Management
info@agoodson.com
www.agoodson.com
Tel +1 514 482 0488

Daniel Egnéus
Via Galeazzo Alessi 61
00176 Rome, Italy
Tel + 39 (0)6 24300929/+ 39 333 2403904
daniel@danielegneus.com
www.danielegneus.com

Christiane Engel
me@desertfriends.com
www.desertfriends.com

Natascha Engelmann
Stratenhof, D-40629 Düsseldorf
Germany
Tel +49 (0)211 9292 580
natascha@engelworld.com

Laura-Julie Griesch
Kirchenweg 68, 90419 Nürnberg
Germany
Tel +49 (0)179 3919 971
laura-julie@gmx.de

Claibourn Hamilton
claibourn@hotmail.com
www.ClaibournHamilton.com

Monica Hellström
390 Hooper St #8B, Brooklyn,
New York, NY 11211, USA
Tel (US) +1 718 302 6940
Tel (Sweden) +46 70 756 5523
hellbruden@bigplanet.com
www.hellbruden.com
Represented in Sweden by Emmylou
Tel +46 8 640 4400/ +46 70 248 2022
info@emmylou.se
www.emmylou.se

Susan Hippe
Tel +44 (0)7939 544326
s_hippi@yahoo.co.uk
www.absolutearts.com/portfolios/s/susanhippe

Amy Howard
106 Main Street, Horsley Woodhouse
Derbyshire, DE7 6AU, England
Tel +44 (0)1332 881966/
+ 44 (0)7971 631428
AmyHowardL@aol.com

Gwen Keraval
28 rue Baraban, 69003 Lyon, France
Tel +33 (0)4 72 35 06 99
gwen_keraval@club-internet.fr
www.gwenkeraval.com

Anthony Kolber
2 Unley Grove, Ascot Vale, Vic.
Australia 3032
kolber@designterrorist.net
www.vectorstains.tk

Luc Latulippe
802–1952 Comox Street, Vancouver
BC, V6G 1G5, Canada
Tel +1 604 687 0779
luclatulippe@mac.com
www.luclatulippe.com

Josie Louise
31a Limes Road, West Croydon, Surrey
CR0 2HF, England
Tel +44 (0)20 8684 3641
josie@warmtoast.com
www.warmtoast.com

LULU*Illustration
Stargarderstr.32, 10437 Berlin, Germany
Tel +49 (0)304 4676 974
lulu@plasticpirate.com
www.plasticpirate.com
Represented by Kate Larkworthy Artist
Representation Ltd.
Tel +1 212 531 1722/ +1 212 531 1739
kate@larkworthy.com
www.larkworthy.com

Sean Macfarlane
7 Longs Court, Crown Terrace
Richmond-upon-Thames, Surrey
TW9 2JS, England
Tel +44 (0)7814 858553
illustr8a@hotmail.com
www.illustr8a.com

Fiona MacLean
6/104 Brighton Boulevard, Bondi Beach
2026 NSW, Australia
Tel +61 (0)29 365 6683
fiona@fionamaclean.com
www.fionamaclean.com

Lucy MacLeod
2 Linburn Park, Wilkieston
West Lothian, EH27 8DU, Scotland
Tel +44 (0)131 333 1498
Lucym050@aol.com
www.lucymacleod.com

Laura McAchon
lauramcachon@hotmail.com
www.laura-mc.tk

Laura McCafferty
38 Tissington Road, Forest Fields
Nottingham, NG7 6PY, England
Tel +44 (0)7799 727988
laura_mcaffs@yahoo.co.uk

Satoshi Matsuzawa
mail@salboma.com
www.salboma.com

Anoushka Matus
Bäckerstrasse 52, 8005 Zürich
Switzerland
Tel +41 78 612 1269
amatus@tiscali.ch
www.anoushka.ch

Richard May
Tel +44 (0)20 7431 4525
info@richard-may.com
www.richard-may.com

Wendy Moody
3 Deacon Court, Woolton Village
Liverpool, L25 5HT, England
Tel +44 (0)7968 592 761
Wendy.Moody@blueyonder.co.uk

Arthur Mount
467 NE Hazelfern Place, Portland
OR 97232, USA
Tel +1 971 645 2481
arthur@arthurmount.com
www.arthurmount.com

Tuesday Mourning
172 Coffey St. #2, Brooklyn,
New York, NY 11231, USA
Tel +1 917 254 8651
tuesdaymourning@hotmail.com
www.tuesdaymourning.com

Sho Murase
Maverix Studios, 1717 17th Street #108
San Francisco, CA 94103, USA
Tel +1 415 522 1717
sho@maverixstudios.com
www.shomurase.com

David Pfendler
49 Carmine Street #3, New York,
NY 10014, USA
Tel +1 212 242 1296
dpfendler@nyc.rr.com
www.davidpfendler.com

Pinglet
317 Bukit Timah Road #08-319 City Towers
S259711, Singapore
Tel +61 415 592 216
pinglet@email.com
www.pinglet.com

Hilde Rubecksen
Livingstone Studio, 36 New End Square
London NW3 1LS, England
Tel +44 (0)7939 285492
hilde@rubecksenyamanaka.com
www.rubecksenyamanaka.com

Marguerite Sauvage
Tel +33 (0)6 17 82 40 29
margueritesauvage@wanadoo.fr
www.margueritesauvage.com
Represented by Magnet Reps
Tel +1 310 876 7111
art@magnetreps.com
www.magnetreps.com

Ben Shannon
533 College Street, #403, Toronto
Ont., M6G 1A8, Canada
ben@shoontz.com
www.shoontz.com
Represented by Magnet Reps
Tel +1 310 876 7111
art@magnetreps.com
www.magnetreps.com

Yuko Shimizu
225 West 36th Street, Floor 5
Suite 5, New York, NY 10018, USA
Tel +1 917 379 2636
yuko@yukoart.com
www.yukoart.com

Anton Storey
40 Hudson Close, White City Estate
Canada Way, London W2 7LX, England
antonstorey@hotmail.com

Ben Tan
bentan@bellefree.com
gallery.bellefree.com/bentan

Eva Tatcheva
Tel +44 (0)7760 224368
eva_tatcheva@hotmail.com

Borja Uriona Uriarte
Tel +44 (0)7743 325645
uriouria@hotmail.com

Kerstin Wacker
Camii Sokak 4–6, Gümüsuyu, Taksim
80090 Istanbul, Turkey
Tel + 49 177 7030 260
henrik@wacker1.com
www.wacker1.com

Robert Weiss
PO Box 87, Somers Point
NJ 08244, USA
Tel +1 609 653 9527
rob@robweiss.com
www.robweiss.com

Fiona Wylie
29 Woodside Avenue, Leeds
LS4 2QX, England
Tel +44 (0)113 228 3884/
+44 (0)7950 932970
fiona@fionawylie.com
www.fionawylie.com

Herman Yap
Blk 107, Bukit Purmei Rd, #02–39
090107, Singapore
yapyc@pacific.net.sg
www.heage.com

Qun Zhou
1056 Summerwood Ct, San Jose
CA 95132, USA
Tel +1 408 272 5520
tracy_zhou@yahoo.com
www.qunstudio.com

ACKNOWLEDGMENTS

This book is for my parents,
Betty & Jimmy, and my sister, Carole

"It was the best of times,
it was the worst of times"
Charles Dickens, *A Tale of Two Cities* (1859)

To the best of the publisher's
knowledge the illustrations in this book
are original, and we have endeavoured
to credit any reference material where
it is known. Should any omissions have
been made, we would be happy to
revise our acknowledgments in any
future editions of this book.

We would like to acknowledge and
thank Eddie Otchere, whose photograph
of Jeru the Damaja from *Lodown*, ed.
Thomas Marecki, Die Gestalten Verlag,
1998 was the inspiration for Anthony
Kolber's illustration on page 5.